FASHIONING FAT

Fashioning Fat

Inside Plus-Size Modeling

Amanda M. Czerniawski

NEW YORK UNIVERSITY PRESS

New York and London

NEW YORK UNIVERSITY PRESS
New York and London
www.nyupress.org

References to Internet websites (URLs) were accurate at the time of writing.
Neither the author nor New York University Press is responsible for URLs that
may have expired or changed since the manuscript was prepared.

LIBRARY OF CONGRESS CATALOGING-IN-PUBLICATION DATA
Czerniawski, Amanda M.
Fashioning fat : inside plus-size modeling / Amanda M. Czerniawski.
pages cm
Includes bibliographical references and index.
ISBN 978-0-8147-7039-9 (hardback : alk. paper) — ISBN 978-0-8147-8918-6 (pb : alk. paper)
1. Plus-size women's clothing industry. 2. Self-esteem in women. 3. Body image. I. Title.
HD9940.A2C94 2015
746.9'2082—dc23
2014024588

New York University Press books are printed on acid-free paper,
and their binding materials are chosen for strength and durability.
We strive to use environmentally responsible suppliers and materials
to the greatest extent possible in publishing our books.

Manufactured in the United States of America
10 9 8 7 6 5 4 3 2 1
Also available as an ebook

To John Gabriel and Eva

CONTENTS

ACKNOWLEDGMENTS

This book was a labor of love that began as a flicker of an idea while on the treadmill and, amid sweat, tears, and giggles, grew into what is laid out here. It would not have been possible without the invaluable guidance and support from a number of individuals whom I must acknowledge and offer humble words of thanks.

I thank the brave women who bare their bodies for fashion. These women are models of how to let go of our fears and insecurities and just live in the moment. Thank you for the work that you do to create beauty amid disdain.

I am indebted to my former graduate studies advisor, Priscilla Parkhurst Ferguson, who supported this off-the-beaten-path research project. I admire her strength and style, two qualities I hope to emulate. From food, to flowers, to fashion, she knows beauty.

Throughout my studies, I had the fortune to learn from a diverse array of scholars whose mastery of the craft inspired my own sociological imagination. They include Peter Bearman, Thomas DiPrete, Gil Eyal, Patricia Fernandez-Kelly, Cynthia Fuchs Epstein, Peter Levin, Ann Morning, Victoria Pitts-Taylor, Diane Vaughan, and Viviana Zelizer. I appreciate the support and encouragement I received from my colleagues at Temple University during the final stages of this project. At Temple, I realized my love of teaching.

My utmost appreciation and respect go to my undergraduate mentor, Paul DiMaggio, whose academic integrity and genuine kindness epitomize leadership in academia. Under his tutelage at Princeton University, I began my first investigation on idealized bodies. I looked forward to our weekly meetings, where I would share any new findings, air my frustrations, and seek his guidance. No matter how severe the constructive criticism I received—with his unassuming demeanor—I would leave his office instilled with a feeling of pride in my work-in-progress. Open-minded, curious, warmhearted, understanding, and, of course, brilliant, Professor DiMaggio taught me how to carve out my own niche in the field. I hope to inspire my students as he has inspired me.

While working on this project, I benefited tremendously from the comments of a number of anonymous reviewers. Whoever you are, thank you for your questions and suggestions that shaped the direction of my work. Special thanks to my editor Ilene Kalish for believing in this project and seeing it through to its end. You pushed me to write with greater nuance and clarity.

Parts of chapters 1 and 3 appear in the article "Disciplining Corpulence: The Case of Plus-Size Fashion Models," which was originally published in the *Journal of Contemporary Ethnography* 41(2): 3–29. I am grateful to Sage Publications for permission to use this work.

While an unexpected death ignited my determination to complete this book, new life moved me to spring into action. Without the unending support of my family and friends, I would not be where I am today. They were my strength when I was weak. When I was in doubt, they were my source of faith. They were my light in the darkness.

I am grateful for the blessing of faithful friends who were my source of sanity during the research process, especially Br. Gabriel, Joelle, Paul, Alyssa, Matt, and my "sisters" from St. Joan's and Lily's Voice who give with the purest of hearts and were simply there when I needed them.

To my beloved mother, father, and Babcia, thank you for instilling in me a thirst for knowledge and providing me with the support to venture off into the academic wild. As a family, we have been through so much in the last few years, but our bonds are forged from the purest connection—unconditional, boundless love. To my husband, Andrew, thank you for reading drafts and providing, at times, much needed distractions and home-cooked meals. You are my rock. To John Gabriel, my hope, and Eva, my precious jewel—Mommy loves you.

1

From Books to Looks

Journeying into Plus-Size Modeling

As the elevator doors opened, the onslaught of hip-hop music and refracted spotlights reminded me that I was far from my ivy-covered home in Morningside Heights. With a quick breath in and a slight adjustment of posture, I headed straight to the reception desk, where a young man tethered to the desk by a telephone headset greeted me. In between answering calls, he shoved a clipboard into my hands with a terse "Fill this out, and give me your photos," and pointed toward the waiting area to my right.

When confronted by a predator, wildlife experts recommend that you stand your ground and not allow the animal to sense your fear. Here, in one of New York City's top modeling agencies, I felt like a helplessly naive sheep that wandered off into the wilderness. The fashion wolves were circling and I was in too deep to retreat.

Needless to say, I was out of my element and unprepared for what was to come. I had spent the last two years in mental pursuits, crafting theoretical arguments, and arguing over solutions to society's major ills as a graduate student. On this day, instead, I was in the gateway to a realm of aesthetics, where the physical reigns. In thirty minutes and two subway lines, I went from books to looks.

This was my attempt to "go native," as the anthropologist Clifford Geertz would say, into a world inhabited by beautiful people, but not just any beautiful people—beautiful fat people. Here I was, a sociology graduate student turned prospective model, waiting to meet with an agent who represented plus-size models. For professional reasons, I wanted to understand how this niche of plus-size modeling functioned within a larger fashion market that privileges the thin body. For personal reasons, I wanted validation from beauty professionals that I, too, was worthy to be among their ranks. After all, being a sociologist does not provide me with immunity against engendered cultural pressures on women to be attractive. We women, in western culture, are always evaluated on our bodies; I was used to the feeling of being judged on my looks.

Clutching the clipboard in my hands, I cautiously sauntered, in the highest heeled pumps that I owned, over to the plush charcoal leather couch. *Look confident, like you are somebody.* Already perched at one end of the couch was a plus-size woman dressed in head-to-toe black. She glared at me as I took a seat. By her side lay a black 9x12 portfolio. I was immediately struck by her porcelain skin and long, thick chestnut brown hair. Here, in this waiting room, I was already in the company of beauty. I flashed her one of my killer-because-it's-so-saccharine smiles, but she ignored me. That brisk fall morning, we were the only two models for the agency's open call.

As MTV blared on the flat-screen televisions mounted on the mirrored walls of the waiting area, I filled out my contact information and measurements on the form affixed to the clipboard. Bust, waist, hips, dress size, shoe size, height, eye color, hair color—my body, as the bass bounced around me, quantified and categorized. I returned the completed form to reception, along with a couple of snapshots my roommate took of me in a faux photo shoot in our living room.

I waited.

I could not help but stare at the size ten, five feet eight inch, sea blue–eyed, and golden honey blonde reflection before me. Questions of self-doubt popped into my mind, which I quickly rationalized away. *Do I have what it takes to be a plus-size model?* How hard could it be to strike a pose and walk down a fashion runway? I was a trained dancer with greater than average body awareness. I often walked in heels down the crowded streets of Manhattan. *Am I pretty, tall, or curvy enough?* I knew I fulfilled the height requirement. I had a perfectly proportional hourglass frame. I was conventionally pretty and photogenic. What about my size? I never shopped in nor even entered a plus-size clothing store. Would my lack of familiarity with plus-size fashions and designers expose me as an imposter? While larger than a typical model who graces the glossy pages of fashion magazines, was I large enough to model as plus-size? *Am I strong enough to confront my bodily insecurities? Am I prepared for what awaits me behind this wall?* Sitting in that waiting room, I certainly thought I was. I believed my past experiences in the entertainment business would guide my current venture into fashion.

At the awkward and impressionable age of twelve, I was "discovered" by an acting coach and soon signed with a manager who sent me out on auditions in the New York City film and television circuit. I quickly booked my first acting job in an educational video and spent the next four years juggling a hectic, nonstop schedule of acting lessons, auditions, meetings with agents, film and video shoots, and, of course, school.

As a child actor, my coaches instructed me to enter the audition room with a blazing personality, to show wit and a high social aptitude. They taught me to analyze scripts for placement of the proper emotional inflection and to memorize lines. At castings, I answered questions directed to me with more than one-word responses, no matter how trivial the question. Through line delivery and conversational banter, I flaunted my purposefully peppy personality. Therefore, at this open call for a modeling agency, I fully intended to woo the agents with my dazzling personality and intelligence. According to my mental checklist, I was ready:

Personality—check.

Intelligence—check.

Professionalism—check.

Guts—check.

Physique—maybe.

Twenty minutes later, I heard my name. A young woman beckoned me into the recesses of the agency, or so I thought until she led me around the corner to a bench in the hallway. Without hesitation or the usual exchange of pleasantries, she asserted, "You are not what I need right now, but here is a list of three other agencies you can try," and scribbled their names on the form on which I had earlier painstakingly bared the truths of my body. The agent made her decision based on the snapshots before she saw me in person, before she called me in, before she spoke to me. Struck by the depersonalized and sterile nature of the exchange, I could merely utter a question about the present status of the modeling market, to which I received another terse reply, "It's slow."

Strike one.

After a disappointing turn of events at the open call, I took the agent's advice and preceded to blitzkrieg the recommended agencies from the list with my snapshots. Two days later, one agency returned my pictures as a sign of disinterest.

Strike two.

Another two days later, I received a call from the assistant to the director of an agency to schedule an appointment. "While I can't promise anything," explained the assistant, "we want to meet you. Bring more pictures—full length and headshots. No holding pets or hugging trees."

"Really? People do that?" I inquired.

"You wouldn't believe."

Ball one. At least I had not struck out.

For the next few days, I watched what I ate in order to prevent bloating, kept to my exercise regimen, and scrubbed my face to foil possible eruptions before they surfaced, while maintaining my usual academic responsibilities. This newfound hypervigilance was all in the name of perfecting "my canvas." I shifted my focus from mental pursuits within the ivy-covered walls of academia to physical ones.

Initially combing advertisements for plus-size models on agency websites, I bravely positioned myself as a hopeful model, attended agency open calls and castings for print and runway work. I soon began working freelance with one agency and then signed a modeling contract with a second. That first open call was the start of my ethnographic account of becoming a plus-size fashion model. I encountered, firsthand, the struggle to rewrite the self, wherein a woman wittingly objectifies and to a necessary degree celebrates her body—a body of curves and solid flesh that is often an object of scorn in contemporary American society. With society regarding models as walking mannequins or passive hangers for clothes, I examined how it felt to be "just a body," a body that was average in society but "plus size" in fashion.

What Is Fat?

As feminist philosopher Susan Bordo states in her seminal work on the impact of popular culture on the female body, *Unbearable Weight: Feminism, Western Culture, and the Body*, "no body can escape either the imprint of culture or its gendered meanings."[1] The fat body is part of this evaluative cultural lens. But what qualifies as a "fat body"? Historians and anthropologists note that fat is constantly renegotiated in culture. Specifically, our contemporary social stigma of fat is an artifact of the work of nineteenth-century dietary reformers, such as William Banting and Sylvester Graham, who demonized excess flesh as an undesirable physical state that speaks to the individual's personal failings.[2] As historian Amy Erdman Farrell documents in *Fat Shame: Stigma and the Fat Body in American Culture*, a cultural anxiety over fatness developed in response to concerns over social status, not health. For nineteenth – and early twentieth-century thinkers, fatness was proof of one's inferiority. Thus, the social stigma of fat served to control and civilize American bodies. Early in the twentieth century, life insurance mortality studies correlated fatness with increased mortality risk and spurred a public health debate whose legacy continues.[3]

Given the concern over improving the health of communities through education and promotion of healthy lifestyles, healthcare professionals developed a preoccupation with the quantification of fatness. The development of height and weight tables produced a new way of classifying bodies into "underweight," "overweight," and "normal" weight categories. Today, the medical community takes precise body measurements through use of the body mass index (BMI), which relies on a calculation based on an individual's height and weight, in order to define "overweight" and "obese" weight statuses. This classification scheme, however, is not entirely a by-product of unbiased scientific knowledge. The boundaries between "normal," "overweight," and "obese" are subject to revision. The move toward a system of classification based on body weight was driven by the life insurance industry during the first half of the twentieth century with the creation and subsequent modifications of height and weight tables.[4] These tables, based on the interaction between actuarial knowledge and historically specific cultural opinions, introduced the notion of "ideal" weight and became a means for practicing social regulation of weight. While the use of the BMI standard for weight classification is not arbitrary, the specified boundaries between one category and another are not absolute, nor are the measurements applicable to all bodies.[5]

From dietary reforms to actuaries and physicians, fat earned a bad reputation within mainstream America. The word "fat," itself, is a culturally loaded, derogatory term. Yet, as a cultural fact, fat is not universally scorned. A fat body is not always a maligned one. For example, Nigerian Arabs idealize the fat body, where, through a practice of forced food consumption beginning in childhood, women work to become fat in order to hasten their marriageability.[6] They consider rolls of fat, stretch marks, and large behinds desirable and sexy. Within the hip-hop culture in the United Sates, a contingent of male artists celebrates fat as the physical embodiment of success.[7] Rappers such as Big Pun, Fat Joe, and Biggie Smalls throw their weight around as a sign of their hypermasculine power. They wear loose, baggy clothes to visually expand their size and take up more space. With a switch of the letter "F" to "PH," the hip-hop community reclaims the term "phat," which references a full, rich body that is desirable and sexualized. Additional terms have emerged to describe this larger body, including "thick" and "curvy," to reflect its more prized status within various ethnic and racial communities.

The nature of size in America is muddled by both medical and cultural discourses. In popular discourse, the terms "fat," "plus size," and "overweight/obese" are often used interchangeably. This is problematic because of the historical and cultural specificity of these terms, which refer to three specific and debatable dimensions of weight. While medical professionals quantify overweight and obese status, fatness is harder to measure. Frankly, fat means different things to different people.

In the modeling industry, determining fatness relies on a viewer's subjective evaluation of another's body. For example, fashion professionals often have strict and often extreme bodily standards. In April 2009, designer label Ralph Lauren fired model Filippa Hamilton for being too fat.[8] At the time, Hamilton was five feet ten inches tall, weighed one hundred twenty pounds, and wore a woman's size four. While the casual observer viewed her as thin, a fashion professional argued that she was fat. Two other well-known models, Coco Rocha, whom the industry considered "too big" for high fashion at a size four, and Gemma Ward lost work opportunities due to weight gain because they could not fit into the common sample size—a size zero—used for garments in magazine shoots and the runway.[9] These cases reveal the range of meanings associated with "fat." Fashion has one standard and medicine another.

For the purposes of this book, I define the fat body as any body that is beyond the norm within the context of fashion, i.e., plus size. Typically, the industry considers anything over a woman's size eight as "plus size." Therefore, according to fashion, these plus-size models are fat.

As the average reader could surmise from a single glance at magazine photos of plus-size models, the basic definition of "plus size" in modeling does not match the cultural image of a fat woman.[10] Most casual observers of plus-size models would probably not even perceive them as "plus size," let alone fat.[11] Indeed, many of these models are of "average" size and weight; retail industry experts estimate that the average American woman weighs approximately one hundred sixty pounds and wears a size fourteen.[12] They are "average" to the ordinary consumer, but, in sharp contrast, they are "plus size" to the fashion industry.

Size four model Filippa Hamilton alleged designer label Ralph Lauren fired her because she was deemed too fat.

What Is Plus Size?

Similar to "fat," "overweight," and "obese," plus size is not measured in absolute terms. There is some inconsistency in the categorization of plus size between the modeling and retail clothing industries, which I discuss further in chapter 3. In light of this variation, when discussing plus size, I refer to the retail fashion category defined by the industry itself. Without standardized sizing practices and the added complication of vanity sizing (i.e., size inflation), a static dimensional form of plus size does not exist. Across the booking boards at modeling agencies, plus-size models, too, do not fit a particular mold. This is in sharp contrast to "straight-size" fashion models, whose dimensions must fall within clearly established guidelines.[13]

While plus size, itself, is a fluid construction that has been created and shaped over time, for the sake of argument, I use the baseline for the quantification of plus size as the woman's clothing size ten, based on the scale used in modeling agencies with plus-size divisions.[14] This practice within modeling agencies does not line up with the retail clothing definition of plus size. In clothing retail, plus-size retailers generally start their merchandise at a size fourteen and run through size twenty-four. Super-size apparel begins at size twenty-six or 4X to 6X.[15] Table 1.1 lists the range of measurements associated with retail clothing sizes.

Generally, plus-size models range from a woman's clothing size ten to size eighteen and need to be a minimum height of five feet eight inches, with a usual maximum of six feet tall; however, most of the plus-size models in the top modeling agencies are size ten to size fourteen. A combination of bust, waist, and hip measurements determine a model's size, as illustrated in table 1.2. Her measurements need to be in proportion, whereas her hip and waist measurements are at least ten inches apart. For example, the industry standard for a size fourteen model is 44–34–44 inches; few models match this standard exactly. Bodies vary, so the measurements in the table represent the most common measurements associated with each size.

TABLE 1.1 *Retail Clothing Size Chart*

	Size 14	Size 16	Size 18	Size 20	Size 22	Size 24
Bust	40-42"	42-44"	44-46"	46-48"	48-50"	50-52"
Waist	33.5-35"	35.5-37"	37.5-39"	39.5-41"	41.5-43"	43.5-45"
Hip	42-44.5"	44-46.5"	46-48.5"	48-50.5"	50-52.5"	52-54.5"

TABLE 1.2 *Model Size Chart*

	Size 10	Size 12	Size 14	Size 16	Size 18
Bust	34C	36C	36C	36DD	38DD
Waist	28"	30"	32"	36"	38"
Hip	40"	42"	44"	46"	48"

Controlling Images of Fatness

Presently, our collective fascination with fat, or the "obesity epidemic," as it is sometimes called, points us toward a body that needs to be tamed and maintained. Evening news anchors remind us that we are in the middle of a fat crisis. Articles debating treatments and preventive measures needed to tackle this much-maligned state of weight inundate newspapers and magazines. Morning and daytime talk shows, such as *The Dr. Oz Show* and *The Doctors*, feature entire episodes on the dangers associated with fatness. Both former President George W. Bush and First Lady Michelle Obama promote national programs, such as his *Healthier US* and her *Let's Move!* initiatives, to combat Americans' expanding waistbands.

In popular culture, the 2008 Pixar film, *Wall-E*, portrays the dire consequences of technological dependence on our physical bodies, where we become fat and lazy folk who sit glued to our television screens. In the film, humans feed on fast food, have robots cater to them, and hover around on chaise lounges to the detriment of their own muscles that have atrophied to the point of immobility. While this is an exaggeration for movie effect, and plus-size models do not match that level of fatness, these popular images perpetuate fat myths and reaffirm contemporary bodily aesthetics. For example, in the film, the advertisements for the latest red- or blue-centric fashions contained slender models instead of more representative fat ones. Even in the *Wall-E* universe where everyone is fat, the fashion models must be thin. Culture, via media, medicine, and state actions, legitimizes ideologies that privilege the thin body and shed an unflattering spotlight on the fat body.

This negative reading of the fat body not only dominates the flurry of images inhabiting the media landscape, but also manifests itself as weight bias in everyday lived experience. As empirical studies have shown in detail, we equate fatness with a lack of self-discipline, laziness, and even stupidity.[16] Experimental studies on weight bias point to the pervasiveness of negative attitudes toward fat in multiple settings including employment, education, healthcare, and the media, which impact the impressions and expectations others have for fat individuals.[17] Contemporary American society discriminates against fat, a point made clear in one study where even fat respondents showed an implicit preference for thin people, as well as an implicit stereotyping of fat people as lazy.[18] Likewise, in a study of health professionals, obesity specialists exhibited significant anti-fat bias, associating the stereotypes of "lazy," "stupid," and "worthless" with fat people.[19]

Contemporary scholars in the field of fat studies, such as Pattie Thomas in her sociological memoir *Taking Up Space: How Eating Well and Exercising Regularly Changed My Life*, aim to confront many of these myths. Some of these include the belief that those who are fat are unhealthy, androgynous, asexual, incompetent, jolly, lazy, ugly, and bitchy. Those who are fat suffer from a mental illness. Fat is unwanted or a defect, a symbol of gluttonous obsessions, unmanaged desires, and moral and physical decay. The fat body is one that is out of control and takes up too much space. Fat is evidence of a failed body project. These controlling images of fat are rife with moralistic innuendos that place blame on the individual and ignore culture's impact on constructing bodily ideals.

For the everyday fat woman, these controlling images of fat impact her relationship with, first, a body that the culture teaches her to scorn and, second, other people who see only her fat. According to sociologist Erving Goffman, the physical body is a manageable material resource that also mediates the relationship between self and social identity, with social identity defined as the reconciliation between how individuals see themselves and how society sees them. Physical appearance tells us about people, i.e., who they are and how we can expect them to act.[20] While Goffman maintains that a certain level of human agency is required in the management of the body, it is society that attributes meaning to the body, which then opens individuals to categorization and classification. Stigma, therefore, is the reflection of society's views and prejudices. In the case of the plus-size model, the presence of "too much" flesh is stigmatizing.[21] Having failed to meet the expectation of a normative thin feminine aesthetic, plus-size models face prejudice and discrimination.[22] They then have the option to either accept their stigmatized state of fatness or do something about it. These plus-size models reject the negative social construction of fatness. They seek to fit into the domain of fashion and overhaul its presentation of fat—a presentation that is inconsistent, at best.

Within fashion, the fat body is nearly invisible and relegated to the niche market of plus size. In rare exceptions when larger bodies do appear in fashion magazines, the images often fetishize the fat body or assign it to a special "curvy" issue as a sales marketing feature. For example, a top plus-size model, Crystal Renn, was the subject in an editorial spread shot by photographer Terry Richardson for *Vogue Paris*'s 90th anniversary issue in 2010. In this fashion editorial, Richardson photographed Crystal Renn engaged in a gluttonous feast consisting of platters full of bloody meats, squid, chicken, piles of spaghetti, an abundance of grapes, and a massive wedge of cheese. This series of images depicts a plus-size model doing what many traditional fashion models cannot—eat. Here, the photos reveal a fat woman at the height of sensual pleasure—satisfying her massive appetite. A defiant Crystal shoves food down her throat; yet, the excess of food elicits disgust from the audience.

Images of plus-size models often fetishize the fat body. Here, plus-size model Crystal Renn engages in a gluttonous feast of spaghetti in Terry Richardson's fashion editorial in *Vogue Paris*, October 2010.

In contrast to fetishizing the fat body, two magazines attempted to use glamour to appeal to a larger audience. Tucked near the back of *Glamour Magazine*'s September 2009 issue was an image of plus-size model Lizzie Miller. The photograph showed her smiling and casually sitting in her underwear. The image itself was only a three-inch square but made quite the impression on readers because it exposed her "normal" belly and stretch marks. In response to a boost in sales and a flood of encouraging emails where readers clamored to see more women with "normal" bodies within the pages of the magazine, the editors of *Glamour* followed up with a photo spread featuring a number of naked plus-size models in their November 2009 issue. The models were Kate Dillon, Ashley Graham, Amy Lemons, Lizzie Miller, Crystal Renn, Jennie Runk, and Anansa Sims. *PLUS Model Magazine* also featured models Emma Meyer, Laura Johnson, Liris Crosse, Wyinetka, and Ivory Kalber in the nude in its October 2012 issue, which was aimed at confronting the topic of body shaming.

The mission of fat activists and scholars, like Thomas, Farrell, and the plus-size models who are the focus of this book, is to challenge contemporary bodily aesthetics that privilege the thin body and to demonstrate that fat can be desirable, sexual, and healthy. Instead of these fetishized, sensationalized, or what one of the plus-size models described as the pre-existing "happy fat chick" image, where a fat woman distracts attention away from her body with a smile that hides any self-loathing, plus-size models want to be captured in images that are edgier and sexier, evoking the pinup girls from the 1950s. They work to reclaim the pejorative term—fat—with pride.[23] They want to exert control over the cultural discourse on fatness much in the same manner that existing controlling images of fatness have dominated their lived experience. I join them and hope this book serves as a call to speak about the very bodies that are ridiculed, marginalized, silenced, and made invisible in our culture.[24]

This book sheds light on the struggle of a minority group working within an occupational structure that privileges a thin body type. Plus-size models fight to get out from the margins and into the mainstream

Plus-size model Lizzie Miller's "belly shot" in *Glamour Magazine*, September 2009.

fashion market. Their challenge is to maintain their authentic voice as fat women amidst a stream of voiceless bodies that flow in and out of fashion's ranks.

As plus-size models engage in a *coup d'état* of normative feminine bodily aesthetics, can they topple the tyrannous reign of slenderness in fashion? To effectively alter contemporary bodily aesthetics and the controlling images that follow, these models need to go beyond achieving increased visibility in the field but to also take ownership of those images. Instead of conforming to fashion's demands, they need to direct them. Their sheer visibility in the fashion marketplace is not enough because of the engendered nature of bodies and the threat of disembodiment.

Disembodied Feminine Bodies

Western consumer culture increasingly views the body as an individual project and primary site for the construction of both gender and class identity. Women, in particular, experience their bodies as not solely for their pleasure and amusement but as under the constant gaze of others, i.e., a body-for-others experience. Our culture places a high premium on the look and shape of women's bodies, as they are visible signs of moral status, gender and sexuality, race and ethnicity, and class position.

Because of the structures and organizations of modern American society, the dominant class, that is, a privileged group with high social and economic capital, establishes and maintains a bodily aesthetic in order to reinforce class distinctions. Sociologist Pierre Bourdieu argues that deliberate modifications to the body, the ultimate "materialization of class taste," serve to manufacture visible class distinctions.[25] This is done by way of bodily forms, modes of dress, and even mannerisms. Members of a dominant class place a high value on beauty because they possess the very resources needed to achieve it—time and money. They strive to improve their bodies and appearance in order to visually manifest their superiority to those who are ruled by needs, not wants. Body image, therefore, is more than a subjective representation of the self but also infused with a calculated objective. For example, a woman, aspiring for membership in the dominant class, may invest in physical improvements and follow a "cult of health" in order to make herself look like the dominant class.[26]

Increasingly, women have gone from being judged on their "good works" to being judged on their "good looks." As feminist philosopher Sandra Bartky argues, the dominant culture specifically constructs the female body as an object to be watched, whereby women discipline themselves in order to achieve modern-day aesthetics. Trapped in a narcissistic world of images, women monitor, invest in, and manipulate their bodies, with beauty as the primary goal. In *The Beauty Myth*, Naomi Wolf argues that "beauty" does not objectively or universally exist. Rather, it is a political tool used to repress women and, thus, maintain masculine domination, as evidenced by the strict bodily standards imposed by cultural institutions such as fashion and the greater magnitude of body projects aimed at women. Western consumer culture directs more attention to the looks of women's bodies than men's. In the pursuit of beauty, women engage in body regimes to cultivate their physiques at the disproportionate expense of their time, money, and other interests.

Wolf speaks of this cycle of cosmetics, beauty aids, diets, and exercise fanaticism that serves to imprison women in their bodies, bodies that continually require new products and procedures to repair any possible "imperfections." The nature of these regimes, however, is culturally specific. While white, upper-class women in the United States may limit their caloric intake and undergo cosmetic procedures such as liposuction to remove unwanted fat, some mothers in Mauritania force-feed their young daughters in order to gain fat and make them more attractive.[27] In a study of ethnic and racial differences in weight-loss behaviors among adolescent girls in the United States, African American girls were less likely to engage in weight-loss behaviors than the white girls in the study.[28] This difference is more striking in light of the corresponding finding that both underweight and normal weight white adolescent girls were twice as likely as African American girls of similar weight status to indicate attempts to lose weight. These patterns of behavior are commonly attributed to differences in cultural standards for acceptable weight among various racial and ethnic groups.[29] Trends in cosmetic procedures also reveal racial and ethnic differences in what is considered ideal; for example, Dominican women request to have their buttocks lifted and Italian woman want their knees reshaped.[30]

Western consumer culture, aided by the fashion, cosmetic, and medical industries, perpetuates a normalized discontentment toward women's bodies by constructing an ideal that is far from the normal, natural body. In the domain of fashion, a white feminine aesthetic that values extreme thinness is the standard.[31] When non-white models do grace the fashion runway, often it is in the context of adding a little "flavor" or diversity to the show; the focus is on their exoticism. This also occurs in popular film, where filmmakers place greater emphasis on the breasts, hips, and buttocks of Latina and African American actresses.[32] These bodies, signifying a racialized exotic sexuality, are meant to contrast with the normative, thin white bodies. In fashion, this image of beauty reproduces hegemonic ideas of gender, sexuality, race, and class.

As a cultural producer with global reach, fashion serves as a "cosmetic panopticon," shaping norms and expectations of physical appearance across the spectrums of race, sexuality, and class.[33] In this cosmetic panopticon, many women experience a pressure to achieve this ideal at the risk of cultural rejection. They become objects in their own projects of becoming. As evidenced by the escalation of techniques aimed at manipulating the physical body devised by the cosmetic, weight-loss, and medical industries, this cosmetic panopticon rewards compliance with a thin ideal and intensifies the horrors of a fleshy existence. Therefore, these women begin to hold themselves accountable for the proper display of their bodies before the fashion police chastise them for their personal failings. They toil over their bodies because they have internalized the sense that fashion watches and judges them for their ability to match the ideal aesthetic. With fashion billboards and magazine editorials as their (th)inspiration, these women often find themselves working toward unattainable goals of perfection, for the icons they aspire to emulate are carefully constructed and manipulated by the brush strokes of master aestheticians and computer technicians. Still, many keep trying, like hamsters on a wheel, because failure comes at a price to one's self-esteem and perceived social position.

Feeling pressured to "measure up" to this ideal, women may monitor their caloric consumption and partake in ritualized physical exertions in efforts to mold their bodies into a desired shape. If they do not possess a thin physique, they, at the very least, admit to undergoing a process of transformation into a thinner, more normative frame, for example, ordering a diet soda instead of a regular one as proof that they are watching their figure, or purchasing garments in a smaller size as motivation for their efforts to lose weight. Many women work full-time to become thin. Their efforts range from wearing control top pantyhose to rein in unsightly lumps to more extreme measures such as pursuing cosmetic procedures at all economic and emotional costs.

The body is integral to the process of producing and reproducing identity, but this obsession with the physical leads to a separation of the mind from the body. In this cosmetic panopticon where we are watched, sociologist Marcia Millman argues that *all* women are prone to disembodiment because "they are taught to regard their bodies as passive objects others should admire."[34] For example, how often do we hear, "My body hates me!" or, rather, at the final reveal after weeks of invasive cosmetic surgeries on television programs such as *The Swan* and *Extreme Makeover*, the phrase, "I am finally the person whom I felt I was on the inside." In such cases, there appears to be a sharp disconnect between the self and the body, and, as a result, these individuals embark on grueling quests to forge an alliance between the two as they work to conform to cultural body ideals.

This disembodiment intensifies in the fat body, where the fat woman resorts to only "living from the neck up." While the thin woman can admire and adore her "normative" body, the fat woman often views her body as an autonomous and uncooperative "thing" that she lives with, distracts attention away from, or tries to change. Her body becomes an object of revulsion. Ultimately, the fat woman creates distance between her self and her failed body.

This form of disembodiment is also common among cosmetic surgery patients, as Virginia Blum writes in her book, *Flesh Wounds: The Culture of Cosmetic Surgery*: "The 'you' who feels ugly is linked to the defective piece but is also imaginatively separable. Partly, this double effect of your body that is both 'you' and replaceable feels like a split right down the center of your identity. I am my body and yet I own my body."[35] Women who perceive their bodies to be flawed attempt to disconnect from their bodies in order to shield themselves from the pain associated with living in non-normative bodies that fail to match contemporary standards of beauty. This alienation from their physical bodies is a response to a hunger not based on biological needs but rather social pressures.

Disembodiment can also occur among women in communities and cultures that value the fat body, as their curvy bodies are hypersexualized and objectified for the pleasure of others. While treasured, they become disembodied, sexual objects. They are reduced to breasts, hips, and booties.

A New Fat Aesthetic?

In response to this engendered objectification that alienates fat bodies, scholars in the field of fat studies call for a reclamation of one's embodiment as a form of resistance against the cultural stigma of fat.[36] This queering of fat bodies is aimed at challenging discursive constructions of fatness, allowing a fat person to "come out" as proud and authentically embodied. Fat activists and scholars desire to reinscribe fatness with more positive meanings and present a counter discourse.

As studies of burlesque and theater performers argue, fat women may achieve this liberation from stigma through the physical performance of fat.[37] Performance, itself, reveals and redefines fatness. For example, a burlesque performer reclaims her sexual agency on the stage. Her performance "functions to support a new, positive vision of fat sexual embodiment."[38]

If it is to have a lasting effect, however, according to fat activist and communications scholar Kathleen LeBesco, a truly liberated performance sexualizes and beautifies the fat body without relying on thin aesthetics. This is problematic because, as cultural theorist Samantha Murray argues, fat women continue to live out, and thus reify, the dictates of dominant body ideologies that they have internalized. According to Murray, "fat politics still privileges the thin body and attempts to imitate it. As fat girls, we still want to know what it is to be thin, even if we do not want to alter our fat."[39] With fat pool parties and lingerie parties, "we simply reverse the kind of response that fat bodies elicit within a dominant heteronormative framework" and "reproduce the obsession with the visible and the power of aesthetic ideals."[40] We still judge women on the basis of looks, not content. We still sexualize and objectify women's bodies, reducing them to breasts and other body parts.

The editorial spread in *V Magazine*'s January 2010 issue, featuring plus-size model Crystal Renn and straight-size model Jacquelyn Jablonski, illustrates this problematic in the theatricality of fatness. The two women modeled alongside each other in identical outfits and similar poses—virtual copies of one another except one is slighter larger than the other. There is no counter aesthetic—just imitation.

Plus-size models play an integral role in negotiating and manipulating cultural interpretations and expectations of women's bodies. In the case of these models, the dominant culture assumes that these fat women are suffering from the "sin by omission," failing to keep up with culturally ascribed, necessary bodily devotional practices.[41] Such regimented practices are crucial because, as sociologist Anthony Giddens explains, in the modern era, we are held responsible and accountable for the design of our own bodies. Following his logic, by all accounts, these women should be hiding in shame. However, they continue to flaunt their curves and strut down fashion runways with pride and gusto. They celebrate the same curves that many other women try to eliminate. Plus-size models

This editorial spread from *V Magazine*, January 2010, featured plus-size model Crystal Renn and straight-size model Jacquelyn Jablonski in matching outfits and similar poses.

provide us with a visual representation of solid flesh that the cultural discourse tries to make invisible.

Plus-size models do liberate themselves from the stigma of fat and embrace their bodies; however, what happens when they are not on the runway but, rather, on an ordinary sidewalk on a city street? Do these fat women still experience this sense of liberation? Do they embody their model personas while living day-to-day in the "real" world? Does this celebration of fat achieve embodiment and create a new "fat aesthetic"?

Building on previous research that has only looked at the staged performance of fat, I focus, instead, on the "backstage" aesthetic labor process. This specific labor process involves all the different types of work a model does, e.g., a combination of affective, emotional, and physical labor, which contributes to her transformation from woman to model. This analysis expands our understanding of aesthetic labor as (1) an ongoing production of the body that (2) depends on preexisting aesthetic ideals that (3) perpetuate women's sense of disembodiment. Instead of presenting a counter aesthetic, I find that plus-size models rely on a labor process driven by thin aesthetics, whereby they emulate a work ethic of self-discipline, strength, and diligence in order to craft an image. They develop a repertoire of specialized techniques to increase their "model physical capital." Technologies of control, such as a tape measure, legitimate and normalize this management of the body capital though corporal discipline. In cultivating themselves according to the demands of their profession, plus-size models engage in engendered body projects that not only control their fat but also reinforce their sense of disembodiment.

By tracing the extension of this labor process beyond the confines of modeling work and into the everyday lived experience of a model, I reveal that, within the theatricality of fatness in modeling, thin aesthetics drive the aesthetic labor process and call into question whether plus-size models can reclaim their embodiment through this craft. Using participant observation and interviews, I document an intensive aesthetic labor process, whereby these models continually develop their bodies according to the demands of their fashion employers. They change their bodies to fit a preexisting image of beauty rather than being empowered in a way that allows them to alter the image to fit their bodies.

A Personal Investigation

Before I crossed the threshold of the agency that brisk autumn morning, I had virtually no experience in modeling. Sure, at sixteen, I modeled in a back-to-school fashion show at a department store sponsored by *Seventeen* magazine, but that was a one-time event and a quick jaunt down a makeshift runway in a suburban mall. I had also been a child actor, but I soon learned that, while acting and modeling are alike in terms of the need to transform yourself into a character for the camera, different skills are used to achieve this goal. In acting, I used my body *and* voice. In modeling, I was voiceless.

Years later, without much preparation or strategic planning, I began my journey into modeling the same way many of the plus-size models I would meet began their journeys—hurling oneself at the mercy of an agent at an open call. I did not have an advantage or an insider connection to guarantee my access. I never took modeling classes where they teach new models how to pose and walk down the runway. I was on my own, alone. It was a huge gamble that, ultimately, paid off, since there was no guarantee that I would be accepted into the modeling fold.

My plucky decision to enter the field as an active participant, rather than a traditional bystander who conducts interviews with those who are involved and watches as events unfold from a safe distance, occurred in a quasi-Archimedean fashion while running on a treadmill—the modern-day bathtub in our body-centric culture. During the fifth virtual lap, I had an idea. *Eureka, I will investigate modeling by being a model!*

Admittedly, I was hesitant at first. Working under the assumption that plus-size models range in size based on plus-size clothing sizes, I did not consider myself as "plus-size"; yet, when I compared myself to pictures of straight- and plus-size models, my body was closer to those of the plus-size ones. It was not until I began looking up information on open calls at modeling agencies in New York City that I learned that my body, at a size ten, could possibly fit the plus-size model mold. I wrestled with the label associated with the possibility of becoming a "plus-size" model. I did not appreciate the cultural baggage that came with the term "plus size." At my present size, I felt neither fat nor thin, but, rather, average. I realized that the fashion industry, as a cultural institution, has power to influence perceptions of bodies and define beauty. For example, after my agent told me that I looked smaller in photographs, I developed insecurity about my size. As a child actor, I was told that I was too big and tall. Now as a model, I was too small. The fashion industry pushes the boundaries of size, with "straight-size" models at a size zero and "plus-size" models beginning at smaller and smaller sizes. Also, I did not know if I had the self-confidence to parade my body with its imperfections in front of fashion's tastemakers. Could I stop fixating on my perceived flaws and, instead, flaunt my body?

All these concerns aside, I knew that I needed to be a part of the action in order to understand both the subtle and blatant demands placed on these women. In this field where flesh is sold, the body is my primary form of evidence and starting point for this ethnographic investigation concerning identity and discipline. This fieldwork involved embracing the embodied skills of my subject.

As such, this personal account of the lived body "under construction" offers new direction in the developing field of carnal sociology, as developed by sociologist Loïc Wacquant. To illustrate, both Wacquant and feminist scholar and sociologist Kandi Stinson offer personal narratives to highlight the embodied experience of disciplining the body under the guidance of organizations centered on the body, whether undergoing strenuous physical training to fight in the boxing ring or containing the visceral shame of stepping on the scale at a weight-loss meeting.

In *Body and Soul: Notebooks of an Apprentice Boxer*, Wacquant makes the leap in methodological theorization and trains as a boxer at an urban gym on Chicago's South Side to capture a form of discipline practiced within an African American community. Wacquant details how a boxer's work extends past the confines of a gym. His level of sacrifice and bodily surveillance involves private matters, such as monitoring food intake, sleep, and sexual activity, and requires a collective teamwork from fellow boxers, coaches, and family members. The boxer becomes "inhabited by the game he inhabits."[42]

In *Women and Dieting Culture: Inside a Commercial Weight Loss Group*, Stinson, by participating in an international, commercial weight-loss organization for two years as a paying member, examines how women continually construct meaning and experiences of weight loss amidst a backdrop of cultural prejudice against fatness. Essentially, Stinson attempts to understand what it means to try to lose weight by actively and publicly participating in a program that emphasizes lifestyle modification and individual willpower.

As ethnographic studies such as these demonstrate, the fluidity of idealized constructions of embodiment that emerges in ethnographic investigations requires acknowledgment of a body that we no longer view as an

object but as an event. In Kathy Davis's argument on embodied subjectivity, bodies are not simply objects determined by culture but rather are
situated in culture as part of the process of negotiating and re-negotiating
self-identity. As individuals, we, our bodies, are vehicles of meaning.

Similarly, I took the perspective of the insider, going beyond the traditional ethnographic approach of observation to step into the role of my subject. I walked in a model's shoes, from castings to photo shoots to the runway.
In this approach, my body became a "tool for inquiry" and a "primary vec-
tor of knowledge" as I learned how to walk and pose and transformed from
a woman into a fashion model. As this study of modeling shows, fashion
places emphasis on what the body can do and what it looks like while doing
it. Thus, a plus-size model engages in an aesthetic labor process that involves
a high degree of self-surveillance and corporal discipline. It is this reflexive
process of "becoming" that only an ethnographic method can capture.

I drew on the physical experience of the plus-size model as fashion
professionals measured, clothed, styled, posed, and photographed me. I
experienced the rejection and omnipresent gaze. For many of the women
I would meet, they depended on this work to craft their own identities
and bolster their self-esteem that had been beaten down by the social
stigma of fat. I could relate to their surmounting pressures because I,
too, had something important at stake—the completion of a successful
research project. This common drive to succeed, irrespective of its roots,
propelled me through the insecurity and objectification we experienced
as models. I anchored my investigation in the concrete everyday life of a
model in order to understand how they conceive of and operate within
a system that, unfortunately, seeks to serve the interests of a client over
that of a model. As a result, this is a visceral insider account that engages
both the physical and mental nature of modeling.[43]

Pounding the Pavement in Stilettos

Armed with my "book" and stack of "comp cards," I actively pursued
modeling work in New York City, recognized as one of the world's

leading fashion capitals and home to many leading designers and modeling agencies. Given its overall prominence in fashion, New York City is also home to many top plus-size modeling agencies. To capture the voices of plus-size models, I entered their unpredictable schedule of "go-sees," castings, open calls, fittings, photo shots, and runway rehearsals.

For those unfamiliar with modeling jargon, at a go-see, a client, such as a fashion designer, magazine editor, or art director, requests to see a variety of models for an upcoming job opportunity. In contrast, at a casting, the client requests to meet a particular model. Agents and/or bookers arrange both go-sees and castings. In large agencies, agents are responsible for directing the overall career trajectory of the models, while bookers handle the day-to-day scheduling of models and billings details with clients. In small agencies, often there are no bookers—agents fulfill the responsibilities of a booker. At open calls, on the other hand, a client will see whomever shows up at the advertised time and place.

At these meetings, the model typically shows her "book," or portfolio of pictures and tear sheets showing the work she has done, to the client. Depending on the nature of the modeling job (i.e., whether it is for print, runway, or trying on sample sizes for designers), the model may be measured and asked to pose for a few shots or demonstrate her runway walk. Before leaving, the model leaves the client her "comp card," or 5x7-inch composite card with her headshot on the front and a series of body display shots on the back, which also lists her personal statistics (i.e., height, dress size, bust, waist, and hip measurements, shoe size, hair color, and eye color) and contact information of the agency representing the model.

Combining participant observation and interviews, I met working plus-size models while waiting at castings and jobs (also referred to as "bookings") and kept detailed field notes. Due to the physical nature of modeling work, I was unable to record observations as they occurred in real time. I carried an inconspicuous, black leather journal with me to all my appointments, but I soon learned that modeling and writing are mutually exclusive activities. I found it a challenge to take notes while having makeup applied to my face or my hair curled, teased, and sprayed.

At the end of a casting session, fitting, or shoot, I retreated to a nearby coffee shop and wrote extensive field notes, relying upon my memory to reconstruct events and conversations.

While in a casting session or on the job, I was unable to conduct formal interviews with models due to the unpredictability of wait times to see clients. Instead, I engaged in informal conversation with them while we waited and then invited them to participate in an open-ended, semi-structured interview either after the casting or at a later scheduled date and time. We met over coffee at a local coffee shop and talked for, at times, close to two hours. In this manner, I gathered a snowball sample of thirty-five plus-size models (see table 1.3).[44]

The plus-size models interviewed for this study worked in a variety of areas. They worked in commercial and catalog print, promoting clothing and products on billboards, buses, magazines, and newspapers. Many worked in showrooms, promoting new fashion designs for clothing buyers at a department store or boutique, and on the runway during designer fashion shows or on-air telecasts for the local news and daytime programs. Twelve of the women worked as fit models. In fit modeling, a designer or clothing manufacturer hires a model to try on garments at various stages of production to determine the fit and appearance of the pieces on a live person. The models self-reported their sizes to me, which ranged from ten to twenty-two with an average size of sixteen. The women ranged in age from eighteen to thirty-four, with an average age of twenty-seven. These plus-size models were older and larger than average straight-size fashion models, who model between the ages of fourteen and twenty-four and normally retire from modeling by the time plus-size women start their own modeling careers. Modeling agencies routinely represented plus-size models as young as sixteen to more mature women in their forties and beyond. These older models generally worked in the areas of fit modeling. Of the thirty-five participants, seventeen identified as white, twelve as black, three as Latina, and three with a mixed-race/ethnic background. Most had some level of college education and worked outside the modeling industry in some capacity.

TABLE 1.3 *Interviewee Characteristics of Plus-Size Models*

Name	Age	Size	Ethnicity	Type of Work
Anna	28	18	Black	Commercial Print/Runway
Alex	27	10/12	White	Commercial Print
Alice	27	14/16	Black	Showroom/Runway
Alyssa	30	18	Black	Showroom/Runway
Becky	23	14	White	Showroom/Runway
Bettina	25	20	Black	Showroom/Runway
Caroline	25	16	Black/Latina	Commercial Print/Runway/Showroom
Clarissa	34	14	White	Commercial Print
Chris	27	14/16	White	Commercial Print/Fit
Dana	31	16	Black	Runway/Showroom
Danielle	23	16	Black	Showroom/Runway
Debra	22	16	Black	Showroom/Runway
Ella	28	16/18	Latina	Showroom/Runway/Fit
Gail	28	22	Black	Commercial Print
Holly	30	16	White	Commercial Print/Showroom/Runway
Jackie	28	16	Latina	Showroom/Runway
Janice	28	16/18	White	Commercial Print/Fit
Joelle	24	16/18	White	Commercial Print/Fit
Kay	18	10/12	White	Commercial Print/Fit
Lea	34	16	White	Commercial Print/Showroom
Livia	25	12	White	Commercial Print
Marilyn	32	14/16	White	Commercial Print/Runway/Fit
Mary	25	14	White	Fit
Monica	31	18	Black	Showroom/Runway
Nicole	26	16	Black	Commercial Print/Runway
Rachel	26	18	White	Fit/Runway
Randa	22	10/12	White	Commercial Print
Samantha	24	14	White	Fit
Sarah	27	14/16	White	Commercial Print/Runway/Fit
Sheena	30	14/16	Latina/Arabic	Commercial Print/Runway
Simone	29	18	Black	Commercial Print/Runway
Stephanie	26	14/16	Black/Latina	Commercial Print/Runway
Wendy	26	18	Latina	Showroom/Runway
Willa	25	14/16	White	Commercial Print/Fit
Yvonne	29	16/18	Black	Commercial Print/Fit/Runway

As soon as I mentioned that I was a sociologist studying plus-size models, many of the women perked up and began disclosing their pro-verbial war stories. At first, some models did not believe that I was a sociologist, since appearance-wise, I seemed to fit in with the crowd. In a follow-up exchange, one model confessed, "I really thought you were joking for the first five minutes of our conversation." More than a few models, upon hearing I was "really" a sociologist, would encourage me to start modeling full-time. A makeup artist at a runway show was con-vinced I was a professional since, in her words, I was "bea-u-ti-ful" and had a fierce walk. Naturally, all of this positive enforcement (which inci-dentally only came from fellow models or stylists and never from any of the agents who represented me) encouraged me to continue my research through periods when I was not booking work and agents stopped send-ing me out on castings.

While getting participants for interviews took nominal effort, fitting into a plus-size model crowd posed its challenges. Often I entered a cast-ing and realized that the other plus-size models grossly outmatched me in terms of experience and amount of curves. Physically, at a size ten, I was at the "small" end of plus size. I assumed that my curves would grant me access into the community since my size was not too far off from plus size; instead, I often experienced the alienating effects, not of stigma but, something that I did not expect, "thin privilege."

At one particular open casting call for a fledgling design firm that catered to a much edgier version of Ashley Stewart's clientele, I was, in blatantly descriptive terms, the "token skinny white chick." Coupling my "smaller" stature with the fact that I was racially and ethnically in the minority, my usual role as marginal insider shifted to that of an outsider amidst a roomful of glares from the other models. Even the two design-ers who were at the casting questioned my presence at the casting. One quizzed me, "What attracted you to this line? Which is your favorite item?" Having peeked at their website before arriving at the casting, I was able to fudge a response, but I knew I was not convincing. I sensed that they were trying to gauge my interest in their fashions since I was not their intended audience, i.e., "trendy, urban plus-size women" who wear a size twelve or larger. My chosen outfit for the day—jeans and a plain blouse—was not a dramatic explosion of style. I did not represent their "eccentric, anti-ordinary" fashion. I was, in fact, too ordinary. Needless to say, I did not get that job.

Attending castings and open calls, I noticed racial differences in my fellow attendees. If I was at a casting arranged by my agency, most of the other models were white, with a few light-skinned African American and Latina models. At open casting calls, the reverse was true—the majority of models were African American and Latinas with a handful of white models. I could not figure out the basis for this trend until I visited several agencies. When interviewing agents at their offices, I observed their "boards," i.e., shelves lined with the comp cards of the models the agency represented. These boards pointed toward the presence of multiple markets within the fashion industry, markets defined by size and divided by race.

It was not simply a model's body size and shape that determined her ability to find representation with an agency, which in turn led to job opportunities. Her racial and ethnic status was also key to determining the quantity and quality of work available to her. High-profile modeling agencies, with access to high-status clients and generously paying jobs, preferred to work with models on the smaller size spectrum of "plus size." They also happen to be predominantly white or light-skinned. This excluded the growing number of prospective African American and Latina models. So, these women and those who wore larger than a size sixteen settled for representation with less prestigious, boutique style agencies that had limited access to clients or, if not signed, attended one open casting to the next in search of work. This racial and size division explained the difference in types of models that attended my castings and open calls.

At these open casting calls where I was the minority, I grew accustomed to the stares and whispers from the other models; however, my token status ultimately served as an advantage. Given that several models did not perceive me as their competition for the job, they were intrigued by my presence and agreed to participate in my study. In the company of these women, I was considered too thin. I had entered some sort of twilight zone where I went from "average" to "plus" to "small" in an afternoon.

Through the Plus-Size Looking Glass

Like Alice, I peered into the plus-size looking glass to find a fantastical world governed by strict aesthetic rules. According to its logic, I was no longer considered an average body type but, rather, "plus size." I followed a path where my body was measured, objectified, and paraded before the public. This book follows the everyday production process within modeling agencies that began with my entrance into the field and concluded with my transformation into a product of constructed images that idealized a larger body.

In chapter 2, I present the faces of plus-size beauty. I discuss their backgrounds and entrance into modeling, as well as their career prospects and modeling ambitions. Chapter 3 presents a discussion of the nature of size in a fashion industry that is clouded by inconsistency and confusion. What is considered plus size in modeling does not exactly fall into the same categorical schema in general retail practice nor match the cultural image of a plus-size woman. Highlighting the cases of the models Velvet D'Amour, Whitney Thompson, and Crystal Renn, I show that there is more variation among plus-size models in terms of both body type and size when compared to the strict body standard of straight-size models.

An examination of the social construction of beauty cannot begin and end with the models themselves. Such an investigation would fail to capture the complete aesthetic labor process involved in constructing an image. The models' agents and clients dictate each step of the production of beauty. In chapter 4, I document an intensive aesthetic labor process, whereby these models continually developed their bodies according to the demands of their fashion employers. In modeling, an inch here or there really does matter. These models face intense pressures from their agents to alter their bodies. In order to work in fashion, they utilize their bodies as capital and embark on a variety of body projects at the risk of losing work opportunities and agency representation. Chapter 5 discusses the agents themselves, the fashion gatekeepers who are responsible for a model's career.

While models are subject to the corporeal demands from their agents, clothing designers dictate fashion trends and aesthetics. In chapter 6, I explore the products of modeling work—the images conveyed in retail marketing campaigns—and a new crop of designers who, themselves, identify as plus-size. This burgeoning field of plus-size designers that self-identify as plus-size women, offer the unique case of establishing a clothing market *of* and *for* their own. As plus-size women, they hold the key to challenging contemporary bodily aesthetics that privilege the thin body.

Chapter 7 explores the impact these various plus-size fashion professionals—the models, agents, and designers—have on cultural representations of fat bodies. The fashion machine hides the backstage labor process from consumers, who never see the physical labors a model endures to fit an image dictated by fashion professionals. Fashion also ignores health concerns. Instead, consumers receive a commercial image of a "plus-size" beauty—joyful, desirable, and free from bodily imperfections.

By examining the complete aesthetic labor process—both the front stage and backstage behaviors—and the relationships between these cultural producers, I show that a plus-size model's performance does not result in the reclamation of her embodiment. Yes, the plus-size model challenges contemporary bodily aesthetics that privilege the thin body, demonstrates that fat can be sexy, and feels empowered while doing it. At the individual level, she succeeds in overcoming years of self-loathing and shame over her body. Furthermore, the entrepreneurial designers who identify as plus size do envision a new aesthetic for fat women. However, the day-to-day interactions between a plus-size model and her agent reveal the model's lack of control in the construction of the image of beauty. At the institutional level, the fashion industry perpetuates her objectification. A plus-size model conforms to an image created by fashion's tastemakers. Her body fits within narrowly defined parameters of *their* choosing. Ultimately, she molds her body to fit an image instead of molding an image of beauty to fit her body. Within this occupational structure, she is voiceless and disembodied.

In this book, I give her a voice and try to recognize her body on its own terms.

2

How to Become a Plus-Size Model

A week after the call from the assistant, I boarded a downtown subway to the modeling agency. As the subway car zipped past station after station, I clutched my bag in nervous anticipation of the meeting. My bag held the additional snapshots the agency had requested that my roommate took of me in a haphazard photo shoot in our living room a couple of days before. A flurry of thoughts filled the darkness of the underground—*Will this meeting end like the last? Was this a foolhardy idea doomed to fail?*

When I emerged on street level from the depths of the subway station, I quickly found the office building and then backtracked to a drug store around the corner. When I went to auditions as a child actor, my mom and I rode into the city on the commuter rail system, hopped on the subway, and then stopped at any fast-food restaurant within the vicinity of the audition location for a cup of standard, orange pekoe tea and small fries. (This was before coffee shops replaced the ubiquitous fast food joint on every Manhattan city block.) It became our ritual that helped me to mentally distance myself from the stresses of the school day and prepare myself for the audition. On this day, I was too nervous for a cup of tea and simply wanted to inconspicuously check my hair and makeup.

I returned to the building promptly at 11:15 a.m. for my 11:30 a.m. appointment and rode the elevator up to the agency's suite. When the doors opened, a rush of sights and sounds did not greet me as in the last agency. Instead, the décor was rather sparse. A mere potted plant and a stand-alone air purifier accented the off-white walls of the reception area.

The receptionist handed me some paperwork to fill out and directed me to a pair of chairs against the opposite wall. I waited, again.

I was sitting in the center of daily operations for this mid-sized agency, which employed up to eight modeling agents. Agents swirled about the facility, scampering from one office to another, often pausing at reception to chat with the young woman answering the phones or pick up bundles of mail. From my seat, I heard an agent haggle over the phone with a client about an upcoming television commercial. Another complained to a client about a delayed payment. The constant chatter and underlying buzz from the air purifier lulled me into a state of complacency such that I had not noticed that an hour had passed. Finally, I was called into the director's office.

I entered. On a desk in front of me were piles of photos and proof sheets. To my left, shelves displaying the faces of dozens of plus-size models with ruby lips and smoky eyes stared down at me. These were the director's "girls"; they were his business. I wanted my picture up on that wall.

Having failed to learn from my previous interaction with a modeling agent, I was caught off guard by a lack of personal introduction. Instead, in rapid-fire succession, Bobby, the director, detailed my fate as a plus-size model while he visually sized me up aloud:

> You're cute and have a good personality but a bit small for plus. We start at [size] fourteen but you may be right for fit and commercial [modeling]. You have good eyes, teeth, and well proportioned . . . You will have to maintain your shape . . . Besides fit modeling, you could do showroom and commercial print for catalogues, cute little articles in magazines like *Marie Claire*, and commercials like Verizon . . . You are more of the Banana Republic look . . . classier, sophisticated.

At some point during his verbal tirade, I reckoned this was a sales pitch to tantalize my model dreams, throwing me candy bits with recognizable retailers and markets to bait me. As much as I tried to sell myself to this agent, he tried to sell his services to me. I felt relieved that Bobby, a fashion insider, thought I might have a future in modeling. The first agency open call left me discouraged, but now I was hopeful, my confidence bolstered. His positive evaluation of my body and "look" was the validation I needed to pursue this adventure. I could do this.

Before agreeing to work with me on a freelance basis, Bobby required that I "test," i.e., have photos taken by a professional fashion photographer to see how I perform in front of a camera and acquire high-quality photos for my portfolio. After the test shoot, we would meet again to discuss my modeling future and "get rolling." He handed me a photographer's business card and directed me out the door. My modeling journey had officially begun.

Typology of Recruitment into Plus-Size Modeling

The nature of modeling work suggests that models are different from the general population. Compounding the difficulty of working under the conditions of impersonality, objectification, and necessary corporal discipline, plus-size models face additional scrutiny due to the negative cultural view of fat. While Erving Goffman's view of stigma suggests that fat women would be more inclined to cover up their curves and excess flesh, these women chose to enter a field where they publicly parade their fat bodies for a discerning public. Essentially, it is this very courage to flaunt their bodies that sets plus-size models apart from traditional, straight-size models. These women shed a penetrating layer of shame and guilt built up over the years to reveal a new, confident self that was no longer afraid to enjoy her size and shape. These plus-size models broke with conventional interpretations of their social identity by flaunting their fat bodies in hopes of changing the cultural discourse.[1]

The typical routes to enter into plus-size modeling include the former straight-size model, the performer, the outsider, and the self-promoter. In the first type, a straight-size model discovered plus-size modeling after she failed to maintain a thin physique. As plus size, she tends to inhabit the smaller end of the size spectrum. In the second, a non-model working in entertainment booked a modeling job because of their status as a performer and then continued modeling after that initial experience. In the third, a fashion insider recruited a woman without any previous modeling experience. In the fourth, a woman entered the field of her own volition without the aid of a network connection. As my own case demonstrates, this is possible but requires a great deal of determination and luck to acquire contacts. Success, by any route, is rare.

Formers

Some of today's top earning plus-size models began their modeling careers as straight-size models. Crystal Renn's career trajectory is a prime example of this route. After struggling to maintain weight as a straight-size model by exercising for eight hours a day, Crystal transitioned to plus-size modeling:

> You know, I was so happy for once, and I was really comfortable in who I was. You know, whereas before, I was completely unhappy, and you know, scared and insecure. It was a whole different me . . . I really learned—it took me six years, but I learned to be who I was.[2]

Livia's story is another example of this transition. While working as a size seven fit model in Los Angeles, Livia's body "gave up" on her due to hunger and dehydration, so she decided to move to New York, where she discovered plus-size modeling. Clarissa, too, switched to plus-size modeling after a couple of, self-described, unsuccessful years as a straight-size model:

> I was told my boobs were too big, my hips too wide. I wasn't booking work and trying to lose [weight] wasn't working . . . I stopped fighting my body and found a new career in plus[-size modeling].

As a size fourteen commercial print model, Clarissa booked more jobs than when she was a smaller size.

In their first stints as models, these formers tried to maintain a thin model body type to the detriment of their own health and emotional well-being, exacerbated by the pressures of working alongside pre-teen models with extraordinarily high metabolisms. They felt like failures as their bodies changed despite their best efforts. Livia admitted that she felt uncomfortable with her body as it began to change: "I believed I had to cover myself up. I was ashamed I couldn't control it [her body] . . . I failed at my job." These formers tried to mold their bodies to match the thin model expectation; yet, in that very process of losing weight, they gained insecurity and body loathing.

Once these former straight-size models discovered plus-size modeling, they found a place where they embraced their bodies and even modeled alongside straight-size models. "When I stopped trying to fit the mold my agency wanted [as a straight-size model]," Clarissa explained, "I entered a kind of happy place. I made peace with my body." As plus-size models, their bodies, which no longer fit the normative expectation of a straight-size fashion model, were valued for their natural curves.

Performers

Another freelance, size sixteen/eighteen model, Janice, agreed with the sentiments of the formers:

> Despite all the problems in this [modeling] industry, I'm rewarded for being myself. I'm grateful for there to be such an industry. I'm honored to take part in this field where I can potentially change minds about beauty.

She was thankful for the opportunity to work in a field where she could be herself in her fat body. Janice fell within the second type of recruitment—performance artists, such as actors and singers, who were offered modeling work and then decided to pursue additional modeling opportunities. Primarily an actor, Janice earned the much-coveted SAG (Screen Actors Guild) card from, to her own disbelief, booking a modeling commercial. A self-described "chubby" girl, Janice never thought of her body as something useful, let alone something that would bolster her acting career. She understood that to act, she needed to be thinner, but as a plus-size model Janice could be her two hundred-pound self. Armed with the good fortune of receiving union benefits, she focused on auditioning for acting jobs, but admitted that modeling jobs were more lucrative and she intended to continue to model until she got her big acting break.

Lea, too, an accomplished Broadway performer, began working as a size sixteen plus-size model to earn extra money. She regularly worked in showrooms, parading in next season's designs for fashion buyers. She recalled, "I thought, 'I might as well try it [modeling].' And guess what? I was the right size. It worked out, and I have extra cash in my pocket." Lea did not expect to continue modeling in the long-term. For her, this was a temporary opportunity that turned into a series of reoccurring commercial print jobs, where she modeled clothes for department store circulars.

Gail, a size twenty-two commercial and catalog print model and singer from Boston, also found herself thrust into modeling while on a whim to bolster her other performance-centric career aspirations. A fan of a custom plus-size design label, Gail added the fashion line to her friend list on her social networking page. The owners of the fashion label, after listening to a couple of tracks on her profile page, decided Gail's style matched that of the fashion's and asked her to model their latest collection in an upcoming advertising campaign. "It was random," recalled Gail, "but hopefully this gig will help my career with more publicity and exposure. I may try acting, as well." Gail signed a contract with the fashion label and divides her time between modeling and music.

Outsiders

Given the similarity between modeling and the performing arts, it is not unreasonable to consider a professional leap from straight-size modeling or acting to plus-size modeling; however, for some women, pursuing a career in modeling involved an unexpected turn of events. In the third type, the outsider, a member of the fashion community—a designer, boutique owner, agent, or another plus-size model—recruited a fat woman into modeling. Unlike the first two types who have experience in being evaluated on the basis of their bodily capital, the outsider may be unfamiliar with the use value of her body and, consequently, need to overcome an initial resistance to hide her fat body.

The majority of the models interviewed in this study were of this third type, the outsider who was urged by others to pursue modeling. While there were those few women who previously worked as straight-size models or in other related performance fields and then transitioned into plus-size modeling, most of the women entered the field by chance. Whether scouted by an agent, recruited by a designer or boutique owner to model fashions, or approached by another plus-size model, these women were introduced to plus-size modeling through someone connected to the industry. For example, size fourteen/sixteen model Stephanie was approached by a makeup artist while she was clothes shopping:

> I was in the checkout line, just chatting, when she suggested I try plus[-size] modeling. I hadn't thought about it before but she made me think. If an established professional in the biz says I should do it, why not?

In ethnographic studies focused on cultural producers within an aesthetic economy, researchers found that a greater proportion of fashion models were "discovered" by agents at random and others entered the field by chance.[3]

This was the case of size fourteen freelance model Becky, who, while shopping, was approached by the owner of a Connecticut plus-size boutique to participate in a showcase:

> A woman just came up to me and asked me to model the clothes in a fashion show for the store. I figured since I already wear these clothes, it

wouldn't hurt. . . . Of course, I was nervous, but it turned out fun. I guess
I can say that I am now hooked.

That first taste of the modeling experience enticed Becky enough for
her to make the leap to New York City, where she attended modeling
workshops to learn how to walk the runway and pursued other modeling
opportunities. Grateful for the introduction to modeling by that boutique
owner, Becky confessed, "If she hadn't approached me, I wouldn't know
that I could model. It's not something I could've imagined."

Similar to the hesitation I experienced while waiting to see the agent
at my first open call, these outsiders, like Becky, were initially unsure or
simply unaware of their place in the fashion industry before an insider
showed them the way. Size sixteen/eighteen model Joelle began modeling
after attending an open modeling call with her friend who worked as a
plus-size model:

> At first, I didn't want to go because of my body issues. She basically
> dragged me to the casting. But it was the best thing I could've done for
> myself . . . After the casting, I saw myself differently. I looked around the
> room and saw a group of plus beauties. I belonged. "I could do that," I
> thought to myself. I really did believe it . . . Finally, I appreciated my body
> instead of hiding from it.

Mary, too, was recruited by another working plus-size model who urged
her to pursue a modeling career. "I was shocked by the suggestion," she
admitted. "I thought only anorexic girls modeled . . . I spent so many
years hating my body that the idea of selling it was foreign to me." After
a few months of what Mary described as "researching modeling agencies so I don't get scammed" and essentially "psyching myself up for
the challenge," she approached a few plus-size agencies and eventually
signed with one. As a result, she worked steadily for a couple of years
as a size fourteen fit model with a few designers. Given the normative
expectation of fashion models as young, tall, and thin, it is no wonder

that these women had trouble envisioning a place for themselves on the fashion boards. All of these women, who were already in their twenties when they began modeling, were older and larger than the traditional fashion model.

Self-Promoters

The fourth type, the self-promoter, was a fat woman who entered the field of plus-size modeling of her own volition without a network connection to aid in her pursuit. Without this help, she was left to her own resources, cold calling agencies and sending in blind submissions.

For some women like Willa, modeling was thought to be an unattainable dream, but as Willa discovered, it only took a few courageous steps:

> I had been told that I should look into modeling since I was a little girl, but didn't think anyone would be interested in hiring me. Last year, I finally took a chance and sent my pictures to "Curvy Clothes," and I've been modeling with them ever since.

Willa was considered lucky to have booked a job on her first try. After working steadily as a size fourteen/sixteen catalog model for a reputable plus-size retailer, she signed with an agency specializing in fit modeling and hoped to expand her modeling career. Rachel, who worked as a size eighteen fit model for a few local companies, had a similar start:

> I had thought about modeling for quite some time and finally took a chance and entered a contest through a department store to do one of their runway shows. I was put in touch with an agency and have been working since then.

Rachel hoped to expand into commercial print work in the near future.

There are opportunities for those without prior experience to enter the field. Many plus-size fashion labels, from large-scale plus-size retailers like Torrid and IGIG to smaller, independent labels like the one in Gail's case, recruited models directly from their customer base by advertising model searches online on their retail websites. Using actual customers without previous modeling experience as models in advertising campaigns is an increasingly popular trend in retail. Besides plus-size retailers, Abercrombie & Fitch and American Apparel regularly use store employees in their advertisements. Casting calls, themselves, can be an opportunity for a sale. At an open modeling call where I met Gail, the owners of the fashion label were selling t-shirts and tickets for a raffle, where the prize was the option to buy any item in the collection for five dollars. The models at the call jumped for a chance at a greatly reduced garment and bought raffle tickets by the handful.

Career Prospects

None of the models, whether freelance or represented by an agency, depended upon modeling as their main source of income. At a casting, I met Nicole, a size sixteen, freelance model, who had been modeling for two years and found it difficult to live on her model salary. "Shit," she exclaimed. "I couldn't afford my apartment on what they [modeling clients] pay me. That's why I have a *real* job." Her insistence on having a "real" job echoed much of the sentiment expressed by other plus-size models, for whom modeling was a fun opportunity but not income-yielding, reliable work.

Though there were a few plus-size models, such as Crystal Renn, Ashley Graham, Tara Lynn, Fluvia Lacerda, Jennie Runk, and Robyn Lawley, that commanded substantial salaries of up to $10,000 a day and booked national beauty campaigns and runway shows for Elena Miro in Milan, these were rare opportunities. As size fourteen/sixteen model Marilyn explained:

> Plus modeling is very competitive. There are less jobs and lots of women vying for them. So, therefore, there are only a handful of plus models that are able to solely support themselves by modeling. Think of how many

retailers there are of straight-size clothing—literally thousands. How many plus retailers are there? See what I mean?

With limited paid modeling opportunities, these models sought regular employment outside the fashion field. Some worked in related artistic fields, such as performance, design, or sales, while others held jobs in the healthcare or legal professions as nurses or paralegals, for example. Others worked as personal assistants or in temporary clerical positions, positions that offered flexible hours and accommodating schedules for those last-minute calls about upcoming castings and fittings.

In modeling, success is financial security, but, these extroverted, attention-seeking individuals also find public recognition—fame—desirable. These fashion professionals want to break barriers. During the 1990s, Emme Aronson paved the way for the current generation of models as the first well-known plus-size model. Emme first worked with the now-defunct Plus Models Agency in New York and signed with Ford Models a year later to become their top, highest earning plus-size model.[4] She became the first plus-size model to appear in a Times Square billboard with Liz Claiborne's plus-size line, Elisabeth. In the fall of 1998, Emme made history when she signed a cosmetic endorsement deal with major cosmetic firm Revlon.[5] She, along with the likes of Kate Dillon, who was the first plus-size model to appear in an editorial for *Vogue* magazine, advocated for positive body image and self-esteem by means of publishing books to lecturing youth in high schools and college campuses across the United States:

> I have a deep concern for women who wear size fourteen and above. They have no voice. My book and my talks are vehicles to say, "You're not alone." Women who've read the book call me and cry. It's the first time they're hearing a positive, nonbashing message.[6]

These plus-size model pioneers relished the limited opportunities presented to them in the beginning. Though, as they were unfamiliar with the territory, these models faced challenges. According to Barbara, a director of a plus-size modeling division with more than twenty-five years experience as an agent, the models were "awful" in the beginning because "they couldn't see past what really could be." Without examples before them, these plus-size models failed to imagine the possibilities; they struggled to book each job.

This lack of vision was not strictly confined to the models. In creating a plus-size division at a large modeling agency in the 1990s, Barbara faced the challenge of convincing clients to hire her plus-size models. She recalled, "Was there resistance in the beginning? Of course! I was hung up on. People were laughing at the idea [of plus-size models]." She began her plus-size division without a single model. By the second day, Barbara secured her first model and her roster continued to grow. In the early 1990s, there were arguably only a total of fifty plus-size models represented between the three largest modeling agencies in New York. Now, each agency represents fifty to seventy plus-size models.

Despite these early challenges, the agents persevered because they desired to change the industry. "I fell in love with the plus girls," admitted George, an agent since the early 1990s. "Straight [modeling] had been done. I wanted to break though the barriers in plus. I wanted to get into *Vogue*, land major contracts. I fell in love with the fight." Some of these dreams are coming to fruition. In September 2013, Eden Miller showcased six looks from her designer label Cabiria Style—the debut of a plus-size line at New York Fashion Week.[7] In October 2013, the fashion capital of the world—Paris—hosted its first Pulp Fashion Week where French designers showcased their plus-size collections.[8] Still, these opportunities are few and, like Pulp Fashion Week, often segregated from the main events like Paris Fashion Week. Given the current professional status of plus-size models in the fashion industry, they settle as the faces of designers in the niche of plus size like Lane Bryant, Abby Z., or Monif C., while Target and Wal-Mart pay their bills. "Work is work and money pays the bills," one agent rationalized.

Plus-Size Dreams

Beyond financial considerations, success, for these plus-size models, is about personal growth and overcoming their body issues, a position echoed by modeling agents. One agent equated her agency's success with her models' happiness and touted that her division is "full of happy girls." Given cultural opinions on fat, unsurprisingly, most of the plus-size models experienced a period of shame about their bodies at one point or another. Not surprisingly, they, like Livia, covered it up with loose-fitting garments and even attempted to correct their "defect" through diet and exercise. Before modeling, they rarely saw the use-value of a fat body and, like Becky, never imagined that they could work successfully as models due to their size. They honestly believed that their bodies needed to be hidden and covered up. The overall level of body loathing and insecurity present in these women before they entered modeling highlights the effects of stigmatization on fat women. Their fat was their scarlet letter. As with Mary who spent years hating her body, these women initially saw only their unwanted, undesirable fat. Yet, once they discovered plus-size modeling and this built-in community to which they could belong, they, like Clarissa, began to see their bodies in a different light and changed their course of action.

After Dana, a size sixteen runway and showroom model, gave birth to her son, she questioned whether she could continue modeling after the pregnancy; however, her fellow model friends encouraged her to carry on:

> My friend told me, "What's your problem? Put on a great bra and Spanx and you're ready to go." She's right . . . When I came back [after the pregnancy], it was like a family reunion. Everyone wanted to see pictures of my son. Everyone has been so supportive. I love these girls.

It took the support of other similarly motivated and bodied women for Dana to be at ease with her changed body. When all else failed, she was able to find relief in shapewear.

For these women, a reactionary process—of experiencing shame to attempting to cover up their bodies to final acceptance—that involved the actions of an outside force, such as the boutique owner, another plus-size model, or "friending" someone on Facebook, shifted their understanding of fat and beauty. Like Stephanie and the makeup artist or Joelle and her plus-size model friend, these women responded to positive encouragement from the authoritative voice of a fashion insider. Without this encouragement, most of these women would never have imagined modeling as a career option. Thankful to the usher who convinced her that she could be a plus-size model, Janice acknowledged, "It's nice to be paid for having this body of curves. Too many girls have eating disorders. I want to be another type of example." These models began as women who entered the field of modeling as part of a larger reactionary process that hinged on an active break with conventional interpretations of the social identity of a fat woman.

Black and Latina plus-size models who differed from the normative white body in fashion faced additional pressures to be role models in their ethnic communities, whose embrace of larger bodies may be waning. Size sixteen/eighteen model Yvonne, who was black, saw young black women trying to emulate the body types of high-fashion models through dieting:

> They want to look like [straight-size] models but they're genetic anomalies. I don't want them [the young girls] to blindly change their bodies to match a picture in a magazine and suffer the consequences.

This shift in bodily ideals that Yvonne witnessed matches what anthropologist Anne E. Becker found in the island nation of Fiji, which traditionally idealized a large, robust body. In her book, *Body, Self, and Society: The View from Fiji*, Becker noticed a shift in bodily ideals with the introduction of western television. In a culture centered on food, within a few years after exposure to western images of beauty, young girls began, for the first time, to think of themselves as fat and purged to achieve a thinner body. The thin ideal espoused by the fashion industry is spreading across the globe.

Likewise, Ella, a Latina size sixteen/eighteen model, felt determined to make a name for herself as a Latina plus-size model:

> This is a Caucasian-dominated industry. When I first started modeling a few years ago, there weren't really any Latina plus-size models. Now, there are a lot more of us, like a huge boom. It's time to represent!

As a Latina, Ella embraced her ethnic culture and strove to diversify the industry. She not only aimed for increased size diversity but also racial diversity in fashion. For models like Yvonne and Ella, their work as plus-size models offers young girls and women from a variety of racial and ethnic backgrounds a counter-image of beauty that is largely absent from fashion.

These plus-size models attempted to overhaul the image of the fat woman as homely and unattractive and replace it with one that they believed was, indeed, sexy and desirable. They attempted to break with conventional stereotype because they accepted their fat. They shed the layers of shame and guilt and demanded that others saw them the way they saw themselves—beautiful, gorgeous, and "curvilicious." Wendy, for example, had recently lost a significant amount of weight and felt more confident about her size eighteen body, so much in fact that she used modeling as an excuse to flaunt her body in form-fitting outfits. "I was unhappy [with] how I looked," Wendy admitted. "I covered up. Now, I wear the tightest, shortest skirts because I look good." Working as models empowered these women, like Wendy, to boldly celebrate their bodies.

Having discovered this community, their decision to become models involved stepping out from the murky waters of a cultural discourse rife with weight bias and prejudicial stereotypes concerning the fat body to become the new faces of plus-size modeling. These plus-size models did not hide their bodies. They became part of a niche in the fashion industry that sought to expose the flesh in a more positive light and aimed to create a new discourse on fat.

3

Models of All (Plus) Sizes?

This work presents the changing nature of the plus-size model as produced by the cultural producers of the fashion industry. A major complication that needs to be addressed, though, is the existence of a vast range in meaning inscribed in the physical presence of "plus size." Let us first examine the case of photographer and plus-size model, Velvet D'Amour. How is it that I, barely considered plus size by contemporary standards, fit into a plus-size category inhabited by a nearly three hundred-pound, size twenty-eight model? Was Velvet an outlier, or were the bodies of plus-size models dangerously "out of control"?

During the thin model controversy of 2006 in which, within a span of a few months, two high-fashion models—Luisel Ramos and Ana Carolina Reston—died as a result of complications from anorexia,[1] Velvet made a splash in Paris with her appearances on the runway in Jean Paul Gaultier's 2007 Spring/Summer collection and John Galliano's showing entitled "Everybody is Beautiful." Velvet was cast in these shows because both designers, known for their use of unconventional models, were looking for character types with a strong stage presence. In particular, Gaultier was casting for his thirty-year retrospective and wanted a "big" woman to represent the one he had used in a show back in the 1980s.

The presence of a plus-size model on his runway was not a new occurrence and, yet, the critics were shocked. In a phone interview, Velvet recalled:

They [the designers] got a lot of negative press for using me . . . It was unfortunate. I felt there were a lot of people who were dissing him for not doing even more, when I don't think there are even other designers who could have taken that risk.

While Velvet admitted that she, at almost three hundred pounds, was beyond what is technically considered plus size, she attributed her stand-out performance on the runway to a long journey of self-discovery that made her comfortable and confident in her fat body.

During the casting for Gaultier, Velvet showed him her book, which was full of photos exuding positive attitude and confidence. One shot in particular was of Velvet in a wet T-shirt that said, "I love me." Her photos and her confidence struck the designer, who then believed that he could take a risk and cast Velvet in his show:

I think that [confidence] lets the designer go out on a limb and take me because if there is any hesitation whatsoever, it would be a catastrophe if you were to go out and flip out or fall or whatever else. It would become a total farce.

Her level of confidence to walk on that runway without hesitation was the product of a long journey of self-awareness and self-accep-tance. After years of trying and failing to adhere to a specific notion of beauty, Velvet, at thirty-nine years of age and nearly three hun-dred pounds, succeeded and walked down the runway of the best couturiers:

For me it was just sort of like an extra added, like, cherry on top. You know, and just to me, it really served to say when you come to truly accept yourself, there's great rewards . . . I think that having gone through that struggle, it just sort of shows you that once you make it through that, there's so much kudos you get after that journey.

This journey involved severe calorie restriction, taking the weight-loss drug Fen-phen, working behind the camera as a fashion photographer, and finally coming to peace with her body in front of the camera.

As a teenager, Velvet considered modeling only after continually being asked by others if she was, indeed, a model. When she finally approached an agency at a scouting event at a local, suburban mall, the agent told her that she, who weighed 135–140 pounds at the time, was "way too big." Soon after this incident, Velvet moved to Manhattan to attend the School for Visual Arts, went on a restrictive, five hundred calorie diet, and lost more than twenty pounds:

> I got down to 117 pounds and went back to the agency, thinking like, "woo hoo, I've done it." They were just like, "hmmm, wow, you are still just too fat." At that point there was just no possibility, you know because I had been restrictive dieting to such an extent that I totally backfired and I would eat like crazy and then I would diet. So it was the whole yo-yo dieting thing that got me fatter and got me sort of more of into trying to accept myself versus worrying about being a model or not.

When Velvet later moved to France to pursue a career in photography, she applied to a plus-size agency as a photographer, thinking that she would have an edge as a fat woman. She sent in her pictures, and the agency presented her with the chance to model:

> When she [the agent] said, "Well, I would like to sign you," I was like, "you have to be kidding me. I am like thirty-eight and going to start modeling?" But I thought, "Okay, cool. Why not? I have nothing to lose."

In a relatively short time, Velvet accomplished what many aspiring models can only hope to achieve, namely international recognition and professional relationships with top designers.

Velvet D'Amour.

Many of the models with whom I spoke gushed about Velvet. As one model praised, "She is my plus-size superhero." After the media storm, Velvet received hundreds of emails from women inspired by her work, as well as from those who demonstrated a strong aversion to her fat. While the subsequent years presented Velvet with a variety of opportunities, including the lead, title role in a French film, *Avida*, which screened at both the Cannes and Tribeca Film Festivals, she still experienced difficulty in further advancing her modeling career because of her size and age:

> You know, I have gone down the runway twice for two great people, but the reality is there is not a massive amount of work for three hundred pound women who are forty years old . . . I try to create opportunity for other people because I know that that opportunity is very limited, not

only for bigger women but older women . . . I think that the reason people admire me is because I give them that sense of possibility. I was able to do it. I was able to break through that barrier.

Given Velvet's iconic runway walk and mixed media reception, "larger" plus-size models faced hurdles in establishing themselves as legitimate models. Velvet's presence in the fashion industry was a statement and not the norm. If the industry considered Velvet a "larger than plus-size" plus-size model, where was the lower bound of plus size?

Between a Fat Chick and a Skinny Bitch

Struggling with these questions myself while I went through the modeling process, I mentioned this project to my close-knit group of fellow academics from non–social science fields. While I stuttered to explain my position within the field of modeling and fashion and the difficulties I faced in conducting my fieldwork due to my "smaller" size, my friend explained matter-of-factly, "So, you are somewhere between a fat chick and a skinny bitch." While everyone's chin hit the table, I understood that this summation aptly described the cultural climate that I was investigating and unveiled the stereotypes that underlie the everyday existence of my subjects. In a society where fat is undesirable and carries with it connotations of sloth and unattractiveness, the expression "plus size" is either misunderstood or unknown. What is "plus size" and how is this term understood among different groups within the fashion industry? Is plus size equivalent to fat?

To elucidate this general confusion with the term plus size, I point to the example of Whitney Thompson, the declared first plus-size model to win the coveted title of *America's Next Top Model* in the television series' tenth cycle in 2008. Since her appearance on the show, viewers debated throughout the blogosphere whether she should really be referred to as a plus-size model since she did not embody their image of a fat woman. Yes, viewers agreed that she was larger than the typical fashion model, but, when comparing her body to their own, they considered Whitney "average" and "normal." Whitney was tall at a height of five feet ten inches and possessed a well-toned physique, but, on the show, she was the "big" one amidst, as she described it, a house full of "skinny little toothpicks."

If the visual image of Whitney's body did not seem to fit the plus-size label given to her by the show's producers, what about using a more objective, quantifiable measure such as clothing size and body measurements? While on the show, Whitney herself stated that she wore a size eight or ten, depending on the clothing designer. In her *Seventeen* magazine editorial spread, part of her prize for winning the modeling competition, the accompanying article noted that Whitney wore a size fourteen. On Elite Model Management's website, Whitney's profile page posted her measurements as 36-inch chest, 32-inch waist, and 43-inch hips. Was Whitney plus size?

It was clear from audience reaction that viewers did not perceive Whitney to have the traditional body of a fat woman; however, from the fashion industry's perspective, she was, indeed, plus size. Tyra Banks, creator, host, head judge, and executive producer of the television series, alluded to the distorted body standards ingrained in the modeling industry when she argued during a judging session that Whitney was not considered "big" except when judged as a fashion model. Whitney was a woman with curves and a "juicy booty," whose mere presence classified her as plus size.

The dichotomy between Whitney and the other contestants (none of whom were considered plus size) competing to be *America's Next Top Model* was striking in their coexistence during training sessions, photo shoots, and judging. The judges applied the same criteria in their evaluation of all the model contestants—the ability to take great photos and walk the runway like a model. Whitney demonstrated her comparable skills in these areas, but it was her differing body shape that made her stand out. Whitney stood out as plus size because she was cast against thirteen other potential models, all of whom possessed the body type

66When I wear a size 14, it doesn't matter, 'cause I look *good* in a size 14! **99**

ON WHITNEY:
Swimsuit, Abaeté;
sunglasses, Cutesygirl.

Whitney Thompson. Tyra Banks crowned Whitney Thompson the first "plus-size" winner of *America's Next Top Model*. Her prize was a feature in *Seventeen* magazine, July 2008. Text reads, "When I wear a size 14, it doesn't matter, 'cause I look *good* in a size 14!"

more similar to those seen on models in fashion magazines and the run-way. In this case, Whitney's "juicy booty" made her different.

Whether a size eight or fourteen, Whitney lay somewhere on the spectrum between a fat chick and a skinny bitch. Did Whitney's crowning as *America's Next Top Model* make a difference and aid in plus-size models becoming more mainstream? Despite winning against straight-size models, Whitney's career remained on the margins of fashion as she served as spokesmodel for plus-size specific brands. What about the photo spread featuring twelve naked plus-size models in *Glamour Magazine* and *Elle France*'s curvy issue featuring Tara Lynn? All of these events have brought plus-size models greater media attention, as well as increased scrutiny. Yet, none have received greater scrutiny than Crystal Renn.

Crystal Renn began her modeling career at the age of fourteen as a straight-size model. Under increasing pressure to lose weight, she developed an eating disorder, which eventually forced her to stop modeling. Once she received the treatment she needed, she returned to fashion seventy pounds heavier and turned to plus-size modeling. Fluctuating between size twelve to sixteen, Crystal was the face of Lane Bryant, Torrid, and Mango, graced the covers of *Harper's Bazaar* and several international editions of *Vogue*, and strutted the runways of Elena Miro and Jean Paul Gautier, among many other accomplishments. She represented a new kind of plus-size model, as Crystal appeared on *Oprah* to talk about her body battles and published a book titled *Hungry: A Young Model's Story of Appetite, Ambition, and the Ultimate Embrace of Curves* about her journey to achieve a more positive body image.

But Crystal Renn did not remain plus size. At the 2011 Chanel Resort show, Crystal revealed her dramatic weight loss and became a target of criticism by the plus-size community. How could plus-size modeling survive if its poster child lost weight? In response, media reports quote her as saying:

This picture that people have created in their mind about what "plus size" actually is. At this point in my life, I would have to have another eating disorder to live up to that expectation . . . Because of my size currently, I straddle this line between the two worlds—I guess you could say I'm a plus size straight size model. I am four inches smaller than a plus size model and four inches bigger than a straight size model.[2]

Incidentally, her dramatic weight loss down to a self-reported size eight, initially resulting from a hiking trip in Patagonia and fueled by a return to exercise and yoga, catapulted her career. With her thinner physique, she booked a steady stream of high-profile jobs, working with the likes of Jimmy Choo, Chanel, Zac Posen, and Jean Paul Gaultier. She appeared in national campaigns for retailers Ann Taylor Loft and White House Black Market. She was also featured in the 2012 swimsuit edition of *Sports Illustrated*. As Crystal dropped the pounds, her publicity and hiring potential increased.

In light of a contemporary cultural climate where "thin is in" and fat is something that should be reduced, melted, sucked out, flushed, smashed, and generally absent, plus-size models face challenges in establishing their place in the fashion industry. So, when a successful plus-size model, such as Crystal Renn, loses a substantial amount of weight, she threatens the legitimacy of the group as a whole. In a media interview, *PLUS Model Magazine* Editor-in-Chief Madeline Jones lamented:

> Once she got down to a size ten she lost the support of a lot of people. We're disappointed because she was our star fighting for equality and fashion for us, and now she's going to their side. It is sad that she's turned her back on us.[3]

This sharp criticism even applies to plus-size celebrities. As one model who championed herself as a feminist pointed out to me with disgust, "Have you seen her? Jennifer Hudson lost weight. She has sold out." Hudson's dramatic weight loss bothered many in the plus-size community. In particular, many criticized her "I Can" campaign with Weight Watchers for perpetuating thin privilege, i.e., the often invisible and unearned

Left: Crystal Renn Before Weight Loss in *Glamour Magazine*, May 2009. *Right*: Crystal Renn After Weight Loss in *Sports Illustrated Swimsuit Edition*, 2012.

advantages granted to those of the desired body size that manifest in weight discrimination. In the commercial, the Oscar winner stated that before her partnership with the weight-loss chain in 2010, her "world was can't," but after her weight loss, she was liberated. Viewers received the message that you cannot be a success unless you are thin. Missing from the ad was the revelation that she won an Academy Award for her portrayal of a fat Effie White in the movie musical, *Dreamgirls*, in 2007.

Jennifer Hudson is another in a long line of celebrities who suffered from Celebrity Wasting Syndrome—a trend identified by Sondra Solovay and Marilyn Wann in which fat celebrities lose weight as they gain success. According to Beth Bernstein and Matilda St. John, these fat celebrities:

> specifically exploited their size to appeal to a perpetually underrepresented audience—fat women. Their subsequent frantic efforts to reduce

their size, coupled with their pathologizing comments about weight, both negated their initial positive impact and left their fat fans feeling used, duped, and rejected.[4]

As Hudson achieved success in her career, she abandoned her ceremonious role as fat icon. In doing so, she alienated the original fan base that supported her burgeoning career—fat and all.

In sharp contrast, when Queen Latifah signed on as a celebrity spokesperson for national weight-loss chain Jenny Craig in December 2007, she was careful not to offend the plus-size community:

> If anything, I was worried about alienating my big girls. I didn't want them to think, hey, she's leaving us. But if I can be an example of loving yourself regardless of what you look like, I can be an example of loving yourself and being healthier.[5]

Unlike previous campaigns that featured the dramatic weight losses of spokespeople Kirstie Alley and Valerie Bertinelli, her campaign offered a new angle to weight loss—the emphasis on small changes in weight, measured by percentages of total body weight rather than pounds, and behavior to improve overall heart health.

These plus-size models recognized that they fight for every job and media appearance. They struggle to gain acceptance of their work. They hope to expand their presence in fashion. At a casting for print work, I met Wendy, a size eighteen model who worked primarily in runway and showrooms but was aiming to branch out into commercial print modeling. While we sat together in the waiting room filled to the brim with a bevy of plus-size models, a young, slender man entered, searching for his appointed studio room. Upon noticing him, Wendy turned to me and remarked, "Look at that guy. Did you see that? Fear. For men, this is either heaven or hell. It is too much [for them] or a candy shop. Surrounded by all this, he thinks we are hungry." By her comments, Wendy confronted the cultural stigma attached to "big girls," whose voracious appetites supposedly can swallow men whole, while acknowledging that there was, indeed, a niche for them, as well.

This incident at the casting, provoked by a sheer look, revealed the tensions evoked by the presence of these women in the fashion industry. These models knew that they were fat and did not fulfill the normative expectations of a traditional fashion model. Those, like Wendy, who chose to become plus-size models acknowledged and accepted this apparent incompatibility of fat and fashion in order to continue amidst the negativity. They flaunted their curves in form-fitting dresses, showed off their legs in heels and miniskirts, and walked with confidence.

These models embraced a mission to change their social identity, and it was a group effort. At castings, I often saw the same cluster of plus-size models. Laughter, as well as the occasional "Hey Mami, what you' been doin," quickly filled the waiting room. As Wendy explained, "It seems castings and shows happen on the same weekend. So, it's like a family reunion. We get to catch up." While waiting for their turn to audition, the models shared the details of their latest job, complained about rude casting directors and overburdening rehearsal schedules, and demonstrated their runway walks for each other's amusement. It was easy to gather from these interactions that this was a tight-knit community of plus-size models, where the models encouraged and congratulated one another on their latest bookings. After her runway experience, Velvet revealed, "Some people, for whatever reason, seem to perceive that I am getting tripped backstage and it's all very *Showgirls*, which it's not. It can be really super supportive." The sustainability and growth of plus-size modeling relied on this supportive community of plus-size cheerleaders. As they saw it, a success for one was a success for all plus-size models. Therefore, plus-size models view weight loss by one of their members as a severe act of betrayal. If a plus-size representative loses weight, she is branded a skinny *bitch*.

On a practical level, however, one model's weight loss was another model's gain in work opportunity. While celebrating the success and gains in status as a group, at the individual level, these women developed a strong competitive drive. These models knew that they were easily replaceable with another body and, thus, monitored each other's weight fluctuations. For example, Janice noted with glee during our interview that her "nemesis," represented by one of the top agencies, had recently lost weight. As a result, Janice hoped to get some of her competitor's lost work opportunities. With a limited number of potential jobs, these models used each other's loss to their advantage.

Thin Face, Padded Body

From the onset of my fieldwork, I was confronted with the nature of size and its meanings. When a modeling agent asked me, "Do you want to be a [size] ten or sixteen?" I could tell it was not spoken in jest. Whether a fit model or working in commercial print and the fashion runway, a model's size, dictated by her precise measurements, determines the quality and quantity of work she books. While a size sixteen or eighteen model may be desired by exclusively plus-size retailers, one that is on the smaller end of plus size at a size ten or twelve may earn work with high-end fashion clients and more commercial print work, both in the United States and abroad.

Highlighting this correlation between the prestige of work and the size of the model, agents from the most notable modeling agencies, which handled mostly commercial print work, commented that there was not enough work for models larger than a size sixteen. As a result, they limited the size range of their plus-size models from size eight to size sixteen, because, as one agent specifically claimed, "that is what advertisers want."

Modeling agents catered to their designer clients, who, in turn, looked at their customers and requested models who walked the line between presenting a desirable image for the customer to aspire to and that which resembled them as well. This resulted in a circle of blame, where agents blamed designers for their model demands and designers blamed agents for their supply of models. Fit model Samantha explained this runaround, "The [magazine] editors told me they couldn't use larger models 'cuz designers don't make big clothes. Then, designers told me it cost too much [money] to create larger clothes."

Still, there were times when the pool of available plus-size models did not match the need of the clients. While preparing for a shoot of an editorial fashion spread, an assistant at a youth-oriented fashion magazine had trouble finding the right plus-size model for the shoot. She complained that "there aren't any models of the 'right size.' They are either too small and don't look plus because all the clothes are black or too big and don't fit the sample [plus-] sizes." In my case, I modeled a size fourteen dress, which was at least two sizes too big for me, in a runway show because it was the smallest available dress in the collection.

It is not unheard of for models to be hired to advertise for plus-size clothing lines while they, themselves, normally do not fit into plus-size sizes. Sharon Quinn, a veteran plus-size model with over twenty years of experience, acknowledged that there was evidence of this size discrimination in the fashion industry, as clients hired non–plus-size models and then added padding to their frames to fit the plus-size clothing:

> Look more closely at some of the current window display ads for some of the major plus sized stores. Notice anything off? It doesn't seem to matter that the models look like little girls playing in their mother's clothing—all that seems to matter is that their faces are slimmer.[6]

This tactic of hiring "smaller" models to wear plus-size clothing raised some eyebrows within the fat activist community. Maryanne Bodolay, executive administrator for the National Association to Advance Fat Acceptance, warned:

> It's common in the fashion business to use average-sized models for plus-sized advertising. Some lines like Lane Bryant will hire normal-sized models and pin the plus-sized clothes on them so they fit.[7]

While not fully admitting to the practice of purposefully hiring "smaller" models, Sharon Lippincott, spokesperson for Lane Bryant, acknowledged that the company used size fourteen models in their advertising campaigns, who were sometimes "only size fourteen on the bottom half of their bodies."[8]

At a size fourteen, Samantha witnessed this practice firsthand when she lost a commercial print job to a "smaller" model for a client that used her as a fit model. The irony was that Samantha was hired by this designer to help construct the very same garment used in the print advertisement but not to sell it in a catalog spread. The designer did not deem her size fourteen body desirable for commercial advertising. As Michele Weston, former founding fashion and style director of the now defunct *Mode* magazine, clarified this practice:

> Most plus size fashion companies produce a line that ranges from a size fourteen thru [sic] twenty-four with a totally different ease for waist, hips, thighs, upper arms, back and bust! When the fashion company builds their line, all the sizes they will carry are built from one pattern that is designed to fit the most common size worn by the general curvy public. Instead of a size eight for a missy line, a curvy fashion company builds their main pattern from a size eighteen fit model who generally is an average height of 5'6"–5'8. When they do a photo shoot, this shoot is happening generally six–nine months prior to it appearing in a magazine or ad. Since production is never completed by this point, they build two size samples from the initial pattern: One in a fit size where they can work with a size eighteen fit model to perfect the garment and one made specifically for the photo shoot requested by the magazine. A model must then be found that can fit the sample garment.[9]

As Weston described, the sample garment used in the advertisement is often a smaller size than the fit garment.

Samantha also revealed that she worked with models who, under the advisement of their agents, used padding to add inches to their dimensions in order to book work with potentially more profitable clients:

> They'll use padding to size a girl up. A girl may be a size ten/twelve but the client wants a solid size fourteen. They like her thinner face but want

a bigger body, so they'll make her wear foam padding under her clothes. It's a win-win situation for smaller models. The model gets the job and the client gets the look they want. Unfortunately, it hurts larger models.

This padding technique, which involved inserting foam pieces that are over an inch in thickness underneath hosiery, allowed another model, Alex, who is in-between sizes at a small twelve and large ten, to change her dimensions for a commercial print client who wanted a solid size twelve or even size fourteen body. "Whenever I get a call from my booker about a casting, I make sure to ask which size they [the client] want," she confided.

As a photographer who has shot for catalogs, Velvet D'Amour asserted that advertisers rely on "smaller" plus-size models to boost sales:

> If they put a size eleven girl in and she's wearing butt padding and boob padding and they sell a muumuu with this girl in that outfit, they're going to get more sales having her in that outfit than they are me [at nearly 300 pounds].

Velvet argued that the capitalistic nature of media and retail fashion created this size inconsistency in marketing. She explained, "They need to create the unattainable because the unattainable is what drives capitalism. If everyone accepted themselves, just as they are, imagine how sales would go down the tubes." This tactic of hiring "smaller" models and then padding them up and pinning them into garments is simply part of a larger process of image manipulation aimed at increasing sales.

This focus on a "thin" face reveals another component of fashion's construction of beauty beyond size, proportionality, and firmness. Thinness is still highly valued. The focus is simply shifted from the body to the face. This preference for thin faces echoes the experience of disembodiment in fat women. Plus-size models like Alex literally model from the neck up since their bodies are hidden by padding. Their "thin" bodies are concealed in an attempt to transform themselves into marketable "fat" bodies. These practices reaffirm thin privilege by using "smaller" plus-size models and perpetuating thinness, albeit of the face, as an ideal component of beauty. These "thinner" plus-size bodies, too, are objects in the spectacle of fashion.

Skinny Backlash

As the high-fashion runway model shrinks toward a size zero, a plus-size model may feel constrained to get bigger. For example, Alex, a size ten/twelve model, contemplated, "Since I am in-between [sizes], I wonder if I should just gain some weight. I keep padding for these jobs. It might be easier if I was a real [size] fourteen." Kay, another size ten/twelve model, also felt torn about her size. Exasperated, she explained, "I know I am on the smaller side of plus, but I was told that being smaller was going to be a real 'plus' for me, instead it's been a curse." Kay was frustrated because she personally knew a few plus-size models who worked steadily and were on the smaller end of the spectrum, at a size eight or size ten, but had not secured representation for herself. While Kay had proved her marketability by booking commercial print work with a junior plus-size retailer, agents told her that she photographed too small for their clients, i.e., in photographs Kay appeared smaller than her dress size, and would not take the chance to sign her. She did not look "plus" enough; she would not pass as "plus size." Fortunately, as a teenager, Kay was not worried about her long-term career prospects. Rather, she focused on going to college and pursuing modeling on a part-time basis.

Some models, however, fall victim to changes in idealized aesthetics, manifesting itself in altered size preferences among agents and clients. When modeling agents scouted for "larger" plus-size models, Sharon Quinn noticed a backlash against "the plus-sized girls on [the] smaller end of the spectrum":

> You're too big to be standard size models and too small to be a true
> plus-sized model . . . It's really a catch-22 and a hard place to be right

now . . . Your bigger sisters are not feeling you because you all (the [size] ten, twelve, and even fourteens) have dominated the industry for so long and now the bigger girls are finally getting a foot in the door and they have way less tolerance for the smaller girls right now.[10]

I, too, experienced what Sharon described as "less tolerance" from fellow plus-size models. At an open casting call, I was the smallest plus-size model present. While waiting with the other models in the reception area, I received more than my share of cold stares. It was as if they were trying to tell me that this casting was their opportunity, not mine. At a size ten, I was not "plus" enough among these "larger" plus-size models.

While a few models below a size twelve booked work in commercial print campaigns with national retailers, fit clients and designers in local markets prefer "larger" plus-size models at a size sixteen and up. I attended a casting where I was told that I would not be cast because I did not meet the minimum size criteria. Some clients refused to consider models below a size fourteen, as they deemed them "too small." Already, the boom in online plus-size retailers has presented more opportunities for models who are larger than a size fourteen. In the summer of 2009, DeVoe Signature Events produced the first Full Figured Fashion Week as an alternative to New York's biannual Fashion Week. Here, the runway show and accompanying workshops focused exclusively on plus-size fashions and all the showcased models wore at least a size fourteen.

Too Fat, Too Thin, Just Right

The "right" size continues to be debated and changes with each season, but the presence of plus-size divisions in the top modeling agencies gives more credence to these plus-size models while at the same time "channeling and widening the gate" of what is considered beautiful. As Barbara, director of a plus-size division with more than twenty-five years of experience as an agent, explained, "All models are gorgeous but now there are more shapes and sizes. There is more cross-over than there ever was." As an agent, she longed for the day when the plus-size division would dissolve and be incorporated into the rest of the agency. Optimistically, Barbara noted that in recent years there were a few models who were shared between "boards," i.e., the specialized departments within an agency that focus on a type of modeling such as runway work, fit jobs, or commercial print or a type of model such as plus size, male, or hand and feet parts models. At Ford Models, for example, Crystal Renn appeared on both their plus-size board and specialized women's image board alongside straight-size models until the agency shut down its New York plus-size division in the summer of 2013. (The agency retained its plus-size divisions in other locations.)

In an industry where "thin is in," modeling agents themselves disliked the plus size label. While agents lamented, they continued to use the term plus size because "it is what the industry calls it and everybody knows it as." The term is vague, as a modeling agent, explained, with an increased level of political correctness: "They're not big. They're women with curves." As discussed earlier, the term remained ambiguous and confusing for both retailers and consumers, but labeling a model or clothing item as plus size possessed distinct meaning. It carried the burden of stigma and complicated marketing campaigns.

With this in mind, agents believed that there should be just models, not agency divisions divided into straight- and plus-size models, as an agent asserted that "beauty is not only a size six." As it stands, the distinction between straight- and plus-size models is based solely on size. The basic model requirement of proportionate facial and bodily features is standard across all modeling boards.

Challenging the necessity for these size distinctions is the Jag Model Agency, founded in the summer of 2013 by Gary Dakin and Jaclyn Sarka, former directors of Ford Models' defunct plus-size division. The agency represents models of all sizes, without segregating them based on size categories. Dakin explained:

We are the first agency in New York that's dedicated solely to women of all sizes. The goal is putting girls of all sizes on the covers of magazines, in advertising, and not stopping . . . The average size of the girls [we represent] is a fourteen/sixteen but there are tens and there are eighteens and if there's a size eight or a size six that we fall in love with we'll take them on . . . We're not going to limit ourselves, because the industry shouldn't be limiting to anybody.[11]

Following Dakin and Sarka's lead, IMG Models (the world's top modeling agency) announced in the fall of 2013 that they, too, will no longer segregate models into different boards based on size. Senior Vice President and Managing Director Ivan Bart explained the agency's goals and potential challenges:

We want to be an ageless, raceless, weightless agency . . . I feel like the consumer wants to see themselves. Sure, there are women who are naturally thin and can fit into sample sizes, and the plus size market begins at a size twelve, but where is the average consumer represented from a size two to ten? . . . We might not win in certain aspects of it and it might take a while for companies to adapt to what we're trying to do, because we still have to work for the industry and if they ask for a sample size, we have to deliver.[12]

The actions of Jag Model Agency and IMG Models signal a renewed renaissance of Boticellian curves and growing resistance to size-specific constructions of beauty.

4

Disciplining Corpulence through Aesthetic Labor

I arrived at the photographer's New Jersey studio for my test shoot promptly at ten in the morning. I lugged bags filled with what I had deemed to be the most flattering and fashionable clothes from my closet and newly purchased shoes with "sexy, thin heels," all hopeful contenders for the four outfits to be captured on film. The photographer, who also served as stylist and hairstylist, and her assistant greeted me with a smile and a hot beverage.

While we waited for the makeup artist to arrive, I hung my clothes on a rack, carefully arranged into proposed outfits as I would normally wear them. No sooner had I finished than the photographer re-sorted everything and instructed me to try on various combinations of dress. While I had proposed my purple shirt with a dark blue skirt, she paired it with blue jeans instead. My ivory sweater and brown jersey dress were separated and the sweater was joined with a pinstriped fluted skirt and knee-high boots. I walked into the studio wearing an old, very pink over-coat, not expecting to use it during the photo shoot, to find that it would be the statement piece in one of my looks. The photographer's reorga-nization of my wardrobe made me question my sense of style. *Am I not fashionable enough? Does my lack of aesthetic knowledge affect my ability to book work?* By the time my outfits had been planned, the makeup artist sauntered in with her suitcase stuffed with professional-grade makeup.

I sat in the makeup chair as the professionals worked their magic on me. They were the aesthetic mad scientists and I was their experiment.

As their blank canvas, I had no idea what was to become of me, nor did they ask me for my input. I sat quietly in the chair, anxiously waiting to see the results of their labor. The makeup artist brushed pink, yellow, and gold eye shadow across my eyelids and a bold red stain upon my lips. The photographer gathered my hair, teased it toward the heavens, and guided it across my forehead. When they were pleased with their work, I was ready for the camera.

Flash.

"Chin up and out."

Flash.

"Tilt your head a bit to your left . . . and hold it right [pause] there."

Flash.

I received a flurry of instructions from the photographer to shift my pose in some seemingly indiscriminate way. I felt stiff and awkward as I simultaneously jutted my neck up and angled my chin down. The photographer assured me that these standard modeling positions flattered the body. Each flash represented another frame of film. Within less than five minutes, the photographer shot a whole roll of film. Each minute the photographer peered through her camera lens translated to at least an hour of preparation in hair and makeup. But in that immortalized moment, I realized the extent to which a model needs to know her body to be able to command and control each minute muscle, as she contorts herself into positions directed by a photographer. A fashion model needs to know how her body moves, how to camouflage unsightly bits, and which camera angles best highlight the female form in order to capture a desired look. I gained an awareness of previously hidden neck and back muscles and that the camera requires subtle movements.

I spent most of the day in a director's chair being painted and styled, so much that I developed back muscle spasms the next day. By day's end, I had become four different characters—the sophisticated Parisian, glamorous beauty queen, schoolgirl with a twist, and fierce biker chick. Pleased with my performance in front of the camera, the photographer assured me that the pictures were "strong," that I conveyed confidence to the camera. It was night as I left the studio. I was exhausted and could not wait to wash off the multiple layers of caked, pore-clogging foundation and powders from my face.

The recurring themes of the impersonal nature of the work, insecurity, and bodily awareness that began to emerge during that first open call at the modeling agency were present here at the photo shoot, as well. When I first gazed upon my made-up self, I could not have imagined the transformation that had occurred—the striking eyes, pursed crimson lips, and hair pulled, twisted, and draped around my head. *Who is this person? What image is being projected? Does the photo shoot capture my true self?*

Looking in the mirror, I no longer saw myself. I saw a reflection of the photographer and makeup artist's image of beauty. While these were my clothes, I did not choose which items would be selected, nor had I decided on how to arrange them into outfits to produce the final looks. The photographer styled the entire shoot from my clothes, makeup, and hair to the location and my poses. I simply needed to maintain several contorted positions while appearing comfortable and relaxed and gaze into the camera lens. The photographer directed me not to smile. There were no lines to memorize, no lines to deliver to the camera. I spoke, but not with words. Again, I was just a body.

From that photo shoot, I understood that modeling work is not only that which takes place in front of the camera but also what happens leading up to those staged moments. In order to model, I had to become the embodiment of style, live and breathe fashion, and make this lifestyle the focus of my everyday. Yet, modeling involved much more than my looks. I needed to learn the who's who of fashion, acquire a new vocabulary of clothing design jargon, and keep abreast of the latest styles and products. Unfortunately, my fashion ignorance was gravely apparent that day when I could not name which makeup brands I regularly used, nor could I contribute to the discussion on the merits of strong pigmentation in one brand of cosmetics over others. Like the models I encountered, I engaged in an extensive aesthetic labor process that involved harnessing interpersonal energy, reining in my emotions, and sculpting my body. This was the real work of modeling.

Given the autonomous, creative, and independent nature of working within a cultural industry, plus-size models engage in aesthetic labor that impacts their work and social identities. As sociologists Joanne Entwistle and Elizabeth Wissinger argue in their case study of fashion modeling in New York City and London, aesthetic labor is more than just a display and performance at work but is "part of the reproduction of the worker for employment . . . and involves longer-term commitments to bodily projects."[1] The fashion industry commodifies the bodies of models as goods for market exchange. Through their physical appearance and mannerisms, models work to embody a brand aesthetic. The aesthetic labor process, which includes a combination of affective, emotional, and physical labor, contributes to an ongoing production of self that extends beyond the confines of modeling work into everyday lived experience.

Unspoken Affective Labor

Agents rely on a split-second visceral reaction to determine the presence of what is commonly called the "x" or "it" factor. This "x" factor is the result of affective labor, which involves the "flow of energy between bodies that stimulates reactions in those bodies."[2] This differs from emotional labor, defined by sociologist Arlie Russell Hochschild in her seminal study on flight attendants, as "the management of feeling to create a publicly observable facial and bodily display." Beyond the emotional labor of trying to charm agents and clients, models engage in affective labor by which they develop "a presence that demands attention, is hard to ignore, or stands out."[3]

Bobby, a director of an agency with more than a decade of experience, alluded to this phenomenon as he tried to explain his selection process. According to him, "When I look at the pictures I am looking for that magical quality. That 'it' factor. . . . There's something about it that captures your attention. That's how I look at it." Another veteran agent with more than twenty years of experience offered her own definition, equating affective labor with a special spark, "a quality that makes her a star." A model engaged in affective labor captures an audience's attention and firmly holds it in her grasp.

Many of the models that I met during the course of my research spoke of this flow of energy. They depended on it to convincingly sell a product and connect with clients. For example, size sixteen/eighteen commercial print and fit model Joelle described how she engaged in affective labor at a commercial photo shoot:

> It was [a] give and take. I was low [in energy], so I fed on the vibe from the room. I channeled it into my posing . . . With the right energy, I don't have to think. The camera tells me what to do.

After three years working as a model, Joelle learned how to tap into the energy present in a creative environment and use it to her advantage, such as when she was tired from caring for her young child at home or when she was posing in full winter gear—down coat, hat, scarves, and mittens—during a heat wave. When Joelle did not arrive on the set with high energy or enthusiasm for the booking, she required the use of another's.

As one agent described, a model becomes an emotional vampire, i.e., one who feeds on the energy of others, for there are times when she has to conjure up enthusiasm for an unglamorous job:

> You're going to wear a lot of clothes that are not you. It might be gross, but, like, hey, it is money. You know what I mean. You're going to try on a lot. You're going to work for Wal-Mart. That doesn't mean that you wear their clothes, but, like, Wal-Mart pays your bills.

It is unnecessary for a model to genuinely like her employers or the work that she is paid to do. A model is hired to sell a product, whether she believes in it or not. Ultimately, she only needs to look like she is enjoying the experience and, as an agent warned, "get the shot in the first fifteen frames." As size fourteen/sixteen commercial print and runway model Stephanie admitted:

> Everyone thinks it's [modeling] so glamorous. It's not. I've worn granny panties, leotards, maternity wear. I wasn't pregnant! I shot an ad for Slim-Fast, and I was the "before" image!

Modeling jobs that perpetuate common controlling images of fatness, such as Stephanie's Slim-Fast booking, can test a plus-size model's ability to go beyond the use of emotional labor and into active engagement of affective labor if she becomes preoccupied with what she is wearing or the product she is selling. "Yeah, I could see it as insulting," she rationalized, "but it's a job. They [the client] paid me good money, so I rocked that padded belly [in the maternity shoot]." Models, like Joelle and Stephanie, fulfill their employers' expectations by capturing the energy in the room and channeling it into their performance for the camera in order to get the shot that will entice an audience.

Joelle also referred to the dependent nature of the creative process between a performer and an audience. "When the crew's on fire, I can work it," she explained. "When they [the photographer and technical crew] are there to get the shot, I can work. When they're just phonin' it in, my job is harder." Performers who act, sing, or dance across a theatrical stage are familiar with affective labor. Once they step foot upon the stage, performers actively engage in affective labor with the audience and their fellow cast members.

When I performed in musicals, the cast always knew, after the opening musical number, if the audience was a good one or not. A "good" audience supported the cast by laughing at funny moments, cheering at the end of a musical number, and paying full attention to what was unfolding before them. A "bad" audience, in contrast, failed to react at these expected moments, leaving the cast in a state of confusion and self-doubt over their performance skills. The cast gathered the energy to reinvent each performance night after night from the audience, itself. Each night the show was different because the audience was different.

Models, too, engage in this kind of energetic relationship between performer and audience. This is more apparent during fashion shows where there is a live audience, but it also occurs during photo shoots where the audience is simply a camera and technical crew. When my first photo shoot required that I pose on a rooftop during twilight on a bitter cold evening in a sheer short-sleeved silk top, the photographer and makeup artist cheered me on with warm thoughts: "Think summer on the beach. The sun is shining. It's so hot." They were well intentioned in their offered motivation, but it was still cold and I desperately tried not to shiver. Whenever I look at the photos from that shoot, I see a hint of a grimace on my face. I had yet to be effective at my affective labor.

Smizing

A traditional proverb states, "The eyes are the window of the soul." For a model, the eyes are the window to affective labor. Affective labor involves the model's ability to emote well in pictures, to work with the camera, and convey emotion using her eyes. Supermodel and creator and host of the reality television program *America's Next Top Model* Tyra Banks offered an apt description of this when she coined the term "smize"—to smile with your eyes and not your mouth. A model does not speak; she uses her body to convey emotion. A veteran modeling agent who deals exclusively in plus size looks for women who "have something inside of them" and "the gift of sharing [that] special quality," citing the example of Twiggy, who was "more than her false eyelashes" and could "communicate the feeling of the period" with her body. A flirtatious glance, a turn of the neck, a soft bend of her arm—these looks and postures are the physical embodiment of what a model is thinking and feeling.

All models, whether straight – or plus-size, rely on their bodies as their sole mode of communication. This requires great levels of bodily awareness; however, given the heightened state of disembodiment among fat women, this may be more challenging to achieve among plus-size models. Joelle, for example, disconnected with her stigmatized, fat body when she was a teenager. "I hated looking at myself in the mirror," she recalled, "so I got rid of 'em. If I couldn't see myself, there wasn't a problem, you know." Joelle's solution to her bodily insecurity was to avoid it. When she began modeling, after a friend of hers who worked as a plus-size model brought her along to an open casting call, Joelle needed to literally face her reflection in the mirror:

> I stood in front of the mirror and looked at, really looked at my body, like for the first time in, like, years. I faced it. I had to see my body. [It was] the only way I could do it [modeling]. I learned to model in front of a mirror.

By making peace with her body, Joelle could look at herself in the mirror and not be distracted by any perceived imperfections caused by her fatness. Instead, she worked with the mirror to find the poses that were the most flattering for her body. She went from avoiding the mirror to relying on it to help her develop her modeling skills.

According to an agent with twenty-five years of experience, this effective communication with the body is contingent on a model "being happy with whatever size she is in." This requires a model to be comfortable with her body and a plus-size model to be comfortable with her fat. Nervousness or body insecurity can hamper affective labor. Lea, a size sixteen catalog print and showroom model and accomplished theatrical performer, confided that bodily insecurity interfered with a photo shoot. "Every time I was posing, I kept thinking about my sausage arms," she acknowledged. "I briefed the photographer about them [her arms], but I was still worried the retouching wouldn't be enough." Lea's fixation on her arms limited her choice of poses, and, ultimately, took away her ability to connect with the camera. Even as someone with an extensive theatrical background, she felt awkward in this particular spotlight. Without dialog or a song to sing to distract attention away from her body, Lea found herself more vulnerable in front of the camera than on the Broadway stage. Her arm insecurity hampered her performance and, ultimately, strained her working relationship with the photographer, who later disclosed to me her annoyance over Lea's insistent worry.

A model cannot easily hide this bodily discomfort. It is displayed in how she moves and behaves in front of clients. One model confessed that she bites her nails, so she never poses with her hands close to her face in order to make them less visible. Another awoke the morning of a casting with a large pimple on her chin. She tried to reduce the swelling with ice and then carefully applied concealer to make the imperfection less noticeable. At the casting, she was self-conscious about her face. She knew that the casting did not go well. "I bombed that one [the casting]," she explained. "I was so preoccupied by that zit that I forgot how to model." While the model will never know exactly why she was not hired for that particular job, she suspected it was due to an added level of personal discomfort caused by her temporary flaw.

Plus-size models, in particular, face the additional challenge of appearing confident while possessing a non-normative body in fashion. Randa, a size ten/twelve commercial print model, experienced this when working alongside a straight-size model at a photo shoot:

> Something was different. They [the production staff] treated me different. The photographer called her [the straight-sized model] "Love" but I was "you in the blue dress." I think it was because of my size . . . At the fitting, there wasn't much to choose from. She [the straight-size model] had a whole rack [of clothes]. They didn't seem prepared for someone my size. They didn't seem to care. They put more effort into her look than my look.

Posing side-by-side with a straight-size model made Randa more self-conscious about her body. She felt out of place and re-stigmatized because of her fat. While plus-size models try to expand the definition of beauty in fashion, experiences like Randa's expose how deeply the thin ideal is entrenched within fashion.

A Tell-Tale Photograph

While a model may camouflage her insecurity at an in-person casting, photographs ultimately reveal a model's level of comfort with her body. To illustrate, an agent showed me the proofs from a recent photo shoot of a prospective model:

> Some people, they're just beautiful but don't photograph well. Here's the perfect example. This girl is so beautiful. She is plus-size. Adorable, gorgeous, but I really don't like the pictures. She was nervous. She did not do a good job.

The agent gave a vague critique of the photographs, but this was because elements of affective labor can be indescribable. As he discerned from the photographs, this model did not engage in effective affective labor because he did not see any sparkle in her eyes. Her eyes were, as he described, "dead." In the end, the agent did not waste time determining the source of this model's failure to produce "good" pictures and refused to work with her.

Modeling agents receive thousands of submissions a year from hopeful models seeking their representation, and they scour through each and every snapshot received in the mail or online through the agency website. Some agencies even hold regular open calls. In order to get through all of these prospective models, modeling agents make instantaneous decisions based on a glance at a photograph. That is why it is important for the model to be able to emote well in pictures. A single image reveals her skills at affective labor.

At an agency open call, I had my first glimpse at what it felt to be "just a body." The agent evaluated my potential to model based only on a snapshot, without a word exchanged. I had wanted to talk with her and demonstrate my outgoing personality which, I presumed, would translate well into pictures, but that was an unnecessary part of the audition process. Agents primarily judge models on the basis of a picture.

Shocked by the impersonal nature of that open call, I looked forward to a scheduled meeting with the director at another agency. Surely, I would be able to demonstrate my interpersonal skills during a face-to-face meeting. Needless to say, this peculiar contradiction confronted me again. As I entered the agent's office, he immediately offered this judgment, "You're cute and have a good personality." Without words exchanged beyond a simple salutation, the agent evaluated my personality, again, simply based on my physical appearance in a photograph.

Sociologist Elizabeth Wissinger shares a similar account of a young model accompanied by her mother seeking representation at a New York modeling agency:

> An agent came out to meet them, and, using a Polaroid camera, shot a picture of the girl, right there, in the lobby. In a moment, it was done, and, after a very brief exchange with the agent, mother and daughter headed for the elevator and their next appointment, or perhaps this girl's big break . . . The fact that it took the agent only a few seconds with a Polaroid camera to evaluate this model, speaks volumes about the criteria for obtaining work in the industry, and what the agencies look for in terms of standards of appearance and behavior. There was no need to actually speak to the girl.[4]

If an agent does not see a "spark" of affective labor in that photograph, the prospective model will be passed over for the next snapshot in the towering pile or the next anxious body waiting in the lobby. While it is possible to cultivate this energy over time with increased levels of confidence, if a model does not have what could be described as "star quality," she will not get her proverbial foot in the door.

Juggling Emotional Labor

Models require a great deal of emotional labor to charm clients while being scrutinized by them, as well as to juggle an unpredictable schedule of castings, go-sees, and fittings. During the course of my fieldwork, the impersonal nature of castings struck me. At a casting for a runway show, I walked into the room to find a three-person panel. Without the customary exchange of greeting, one on the panel ordered, "Straight walk twice, no turns. Go!" On cue, the music started and I began my walk down an imaginary runway. The cold reception from the panel left me a bit stunned and befuddled, so, consequently, I forgot to monitor my facial expression while my hips were swinging to the rhythm of the music. I failed to maintain my composure given an unexpected interaction with casting. I let my emotions get the better of me. I did not get the job.

At another casting, I met Wendy, a size eighteen model who had been working in runway and showroom for a women's plus-size clothing store. She recounted to me her earlier run-in at a casting that same morning:

> I got there fifteen minutes early, so I stuck my head in the door and asked if I could go in. One of the casting directors barked back at me, "We will start at noon." But I had asked the director of the show if I could come by earlier because I had this casting and he said yes. I waited until noon and stuck my head in again, and they said they were not ready. As I was sitting there I could hear the casting director complaining, "Don't these models know that noon means noon." I was so mad that I left without auditioning. I pride myself on being punctual.

Unfortunately, Wendy was not able to rein in her feelings for the casting, but the comments she overheard from the casting director revealed a lopsided opportunity structure. Models aim to please clients and casting directors, i.e., to be voiceless, smiling bodies.

Besides the occasional chilling experience at castings, plus-size models also negotiate any unexpected demands that emerge. When I met Dana, a size sixteen model, she struggled with a schedule filled with multiple rehearsals for an upcoming runway show, difficult directors, and hidden costs for walking the runway. Exasperated, Dana explained, "I have to sell forty-dollar tickets to a [runway] show that I am not being paid for, and he [the director] won't return my damn calls." Plus-size models inhabit a low-status niche in fashion. Consequently, fashion directors often require them to sell tickets for runway shows that they participate in. Dana arrived to a casting heavily burdened by these responsibilities (as well as those of a mother to a rambunctious toddler) but, for the sake of her career, she let her frustration pass before entering the audition room. "I'm a professional. I do my job," Dana told me before heading into the casting room. Always engaged in emotional labor, models must leave negative attitudes and low energy at the door in order to perform and impress clients and casting directors.

Another significant component of emotional labor is confidence. This did not mean that these women have perfect body images. In an interview with *PLUS Model Magazine*, Angellika, who had worked in the industry for more than a decade and was the first plus-size model inducted into the Modeling Hall of Fame, revealed, "Do I have things I don't like on my body? Of course [stomach] but I enhance everything else about myself and roll with the punches."[5] Likewise, Joelle vented about a surmounting social pressure she faced to be a modern-day body ambassador brimming with self-confidence:

> People always expect us to be on and confident, but everyone has some sort of insecurity. I still get nervous today when I'm going to a casting. Who will be there? What will they ask me to do? What will I have to wear? I'm like any woman, and nothing brings out a girl's insecurity like a bathing suit. I won't wear it in public, but, on a closed set for a job, I'll do it. I'll be brave.

These models are told to "work it" by embracing their bodies and embodying confidence; however, they work in a professional environment that aims for physical perfection and criticizes those bodies that fail to measure up.

Models engage in the most taxing form of emotional labor when they try to maintain composure while receiving criticism, some of which can be unwarranted and destructive. Early in her career, Janice, a size sixteen/eighteen commercial print and fit model, signed with an agent at an agency specializing in plus-size models:

> She [the agent] told me to change my hair, weight. She even suggested I get a chin implant! . . . She'd call me at all hours, in the middle of the night . . . After a casting, she'd call me to tell me what the client said, like, "She's not pretty enough." Like that helps!

Since a model depends on her agent to find her work and negotiate with clients on her behalf, she often finds herself in a predicament to appease her agent's demands. Under an exclusive contract with this agent, Janice suffered the verbal abuse. Janice acknowledged that her body was not the one typically celebrated in American culture, but to have her agent, whom she believed would be her mentor in the field, was discouraging. "She [the agent] played me," Janice vented. Since then, she has been wary of exclusive contracts with agencies.

A model endures the careful management of her feelings and strain to her self-esteem in order to work from day to day, client to client. Most often, though, these models never find out why they were not cast for a particular job. When one model asked her booker the outcome of a casting, she was told, in vague terms that the client "went in another direction." Stephanie explained, "I'm constantly told, 'You're too big or small.' It ain't easy to hear. That's the business. I chose to do this so I have to live with it." Despite this uncertainty, they persist from one casting to the next in hopes of booking work. Their persistence, despite this unknown, is a key component of their emotional labor.

Self-Surveillance with a Tape Measure

Models spend a majority of their time engaged in physical labor to keep their bodies camera-ready. A model prepares her body for the performance of modeling. As post-structuralist feminist philosopher Judith

Butler argues, gender is a performative accomplishment, i.e., an identity constructed through daily actions and use of the body that culminates in an impression of one's gender.[6] In "doing gender," individuals act at the risk of assessment, where others will hold them accountable for their behavior.[7] Here, the plus-size model, as a gendered woman, is under considerable cultural pressure to "do looks." Additionally, she is directed by her agency to give a specific gendered performance that conveys the impression that she is, indeed, a model. Her job is to use her body to strike the right pose and sell a garment for a client. In order to effectively do so, a model regulates and disciplines her body. By way of toning and shaping her body through diet and exercise or artificial enhancements, the model prepares her body for the needs of clients. These performative acts of a model may appear to be the result of personal choice, but they work within the confines of an existing cultural structure that awards compliance to a constructed image of plus-size beauty.

According to French philosopher and social theorist Michel Foucault, power relations define the body in economic terms as both a productive body and a subjected body. Here in this Foucauldian view, the bodies of fashion models are subject to an agent's gaze. The fashion industry commodifies a model's body, where each curve determines her economic potential. Consequently, a model tracks her measurements and engages in a number of bodily practices to remain competitive in the field.

A Foucauldian analysis of the body involves mapping the power relations that operate within institutions and ripple down to the individual, affecting daily practices. In this case, the specialization of the modeling industry allows agents to categorize models, subjecting the body to classification. Plus-size models respond to this subjectification by the industry by internalizing the gaze and engaging in new forms of self-discipline. Here, the tape measure is an institutionalized tool of regulation as it measures and evaluates a model's body. No longer confined to the sole possession of an agent or a fashion designer, models also use a tape measure to track their bodies. Working within this web of power relations, models become "docile" bodies to fit the desired image of a plus-size model.

Appearance plays a key role in gendered subjectivity, where "doing looks" is integral to the production of gendered social identity. Susan Bordo, in Foucauldian fashion with a feminist twist, acknowledges the productive role women have in bodily pursuits but ultimately concedes that they become "docile" bodies disciplined to survey and improve their bodies, duped into adhering to idealized constructions of feminine embodiment discursively mediated by the culture through a cosmetic panopticon. An internalized sense of disciplinary power, exercised by self-surveillance and self-policing, maintains a model's gendered subjectivity, resulting in her pursuit of an aesthetic ideal established by fashion. These models internalize a normalizing gaze and, by use of individualized disciplinary practices, reproduce the "subjected and practiced bodies, 'docile' bodies."[8] Here, these models actively work on their bodies to achieve a look mandated by the cosmetic panopticon. They judge their bodies through fashion's eyes and according to fashion's criteria. When they fail, they experience a sense of shame and insecurity, similar to that of Caroline.

While a group of plus-size models and I waited in the hallway for an open call with an agency, one freelance, size sixteen model, Caroline, anxiously asked the departing models if they had been measured by the agent during the interview. Once Caroline heard that the agent measured the other models "in over a dozen places no one would expect," she turned to me in noticeable panic, explaining that her measurements had changed from the ones listed on her composite card—a model's business card—since she had gained weight over the holidays.

Caroline knew it was common practice for agents to measure models. The act of being measured, itself, did not trouble her. Rather, Caroline feared that the agent would chastise her for her failure to maintain her bodily measurements. Caroline believed that the agent would then perceive her as unprofessional and, therefore, refuse to work with her. Caroline depended on securing this agent's representation to provide her with work opportunities. As a freelance model, she exhausted her existing contacts and needed new clients. This level of fear-laden bodily consciousness that Caroline exhibited is not only typical but also necessary for a plus-size model, who is subject to fashion's gaze. Models, like Caroline, experience an overt, constant pressure to maintain their figures, since there is always someone, whether an agent or client, present with a tape measure.

Little did I know that my decision to model had an effect on aspects of my life thought to be unfazed by fashion's trends and preoccupation with appearance. For example, I reflected more on what I wore to the classroom to teach a class of college undergraduates. I utilized some of the tricks I learned from makeup artists and hair stylists and gained a newfound appreciation for Velcro rollers. I stuck to my six-day-a-week exercise routine of Pilates and cardio on the treadmill and, with due hypervigilance, counted calories and monitored portion sizes using smaller plates and mini snack bowls. Failure to do so would induce a pang of guilt and lead to stress, which would lead to breakouts, so I leaned on meditative prayer and flexibility training with its relaxing stretches as my stabilizing crutch after the time spent dwelling on my body and appearance. I had successfully internalized the self-surveillance and discipline required of models by a fashion institution. I, too, succumbed to the pressure of tracking my body's measurements daily with a measuring tape, the prominent tool of institutionalized corporal discipline and regulation.

Artful Manipulations

Contrary to cultural perceptions of fat women, plus-size models are disciplined and engage in constant monitoring and management of their bodily capital. Sociologist Loïc Wacquant utilizes the case of the boxer to explain this concept of bodily capital:

> The successful pursuit of a career [in boxing] . . . presupposes a rigorous
> management of the body, a meticulous maintenance of each one of its

parts, an attention of every moment, in and out of the ring, to its proper functioning and protection. . . . The pugilist's body is at once the *tool* of his work—an offensive weapon and defensive shield—and the *target* of his opponent.[9]

Here, the boxer's body is a form of commodified physical capital, requiring monitoring and training in order to win a match.

In this way, bodily capital becomes essential to the boxer's habitus, a bodily state of being that is both a medium and outcome of social practice. Both Wacquant's boxers and the plus-size models in this study convert their bodily capital, i.e., the shape and active capacity of a body, into economic capital. For the plus-size model, her body is her career. The condition of her body—the size, shape, and muscle tone—determines her chances for employment.

Training the body increases its utility and capital. In their ethnographic study of aging ballet dancers, Steven P. Wainwright and Bryan S. Turner refine Bourdieu's concept of bodily capital. To better describe the athletic nature of the professional dancer, Wainwright and Turner divide the concept of "athletic physical capital" into four criteria: speed, strength, stamina, and suppleness. All four aspects are present in athletes with differing levels of concentrated development. While a dancer may focus on increasing suppleness, a boxer will train to increase strength and speed.

Modeling is similar to these fields, as well as to sex work and acting, which focus on engendered physical capital, where a worker commodifies her body. For example, both sex workers and fashion models modify their physical appearance to achieve a successful performance of the body. As sociologists Jennifer K. Wesely and Alexandra G. Murphy argue in their independent ethnographic studies, exotic dancers manipulate their bodies via numerous body technologies to prepare themselves for their public performance as sexualized bodies for male clients. For example, it is not uncommon for an exotic dancer to undergo breast augmentation to achieve the "Barbie doll" body and receive more attention and money from her clients.

Likewise, the models in this study undertook rigorous and meticulous means to manage their bodily capital and trained to increase what I call their "model physical capital," measured by body size and shape, runway walk, posing ability, and photogenic features. They cared for their bodies to maintain their buxom figures and participated in ritualistic skin care and grooming regimens. While photographic retouching eliminates the occasional pimple, a model's complexion needed to be clear and washed thoroughly after a day on set wearing professional-grade makeup. They invested in their smile, straightening and whitening their teeth. Most turned to artificial bodily enhancements, such as body shapers and padding, to achieve a desired, proportionate figure.

For models with less than ideal proportions, Larissa Laurel for *PLUS Model Magazine* explained a trick of the modeling trade:

> Some models, like me, are blessed with big bottoms, but our bust is on the smaller size. So, do you know what we do? We stuff our bras with the pillow cups which we lovingly refer to as "chicken cutlets." One model I personally know wears a padded panty to help her rear end look fuller.[10]

While padding may be used to offer extensive remodeling and even gain in overall body size, most models resorted to minor alterations. For example, one model revealed that she secured shoulder pads onto her hips in order to add inches to her measurements. For models, body proportions were more important than size, so they used artificial aids, such as "chicken cutlets," body shapers such as the popular Spanx, or shoulder pads in unexpected places. These plus-size models artfully manipulated their bodies to achieve the "ideal" body.

These plus-size fashion models possessed great bodily awareness. They attended classes to learn how to walk, turn, and pose. Several of the models that I interviewed attended The Plus Academy, the first training program designed exclusively for plus-size models by former plus-size model Gwendolyn DeVoe. Others painstakingly analyzed the proofs from their test shoot to see which poses best suited their bodies. They knew how to put together an outfit that would flatter the appropriate curves. For each casting, they dressed to impress the casting director. Clients expected these models to wear shapeware (foundation garments worn underneath clothing that slim, flatten, and enhance different areas of the body including the bust, waist, buttocks, hips, and thighs to create a clean silhouette) underneath a stylish, figure-flattering outfit, wear two- to three-inch heels, and generally "be runway ready" with "a touch of gloss and slick hair."

Focusing on aesthetics, conservative styles dominate the plus-size field, so the models need to present themselves in a conservative, neat manner. Agents strongly discouraged models from getting tattoos and excessive piercings. I overheard an agent yell at a model over an unsanctioned piercing. Samantha admitted that she had her ear cartilage pierced but that she never wore her earrings to a casting for fear that it would leave the wrong impression with a casting director. Hairstyles and manicures, too, needed to be conservatively styled and polished, i.e., hair should be a medium to long length and nails should be short and polished with a discrete clear or nude color. Ultimately, agents stripped their models of the freedom to express their individuality through the presentation of their own bodies. This prevents models from contributing to the construction of beauty since they are no longer in control of their personal aesthetics.

Controlling Appetites and Battling Eating Disorders

Maintaining their model physical capital required self-monitoring and discipline; yet, these models acknowledged the role their appetites played in creating their voluptuous figures and insisted to me that they regularly ate a balanced diet and routinely exercised. As size sixteen commercial print and runway model Nicole told me, "Girl, you know I have to exercise because I love to eat!" With pride, she distanced herself from straight-size models: "I enjoy myself. I go out with friends. We drink. I don't have to starve myself." She also clarified, "I'm a big girl, but I keep active. I ran a 5K last year. One day I'll do the marathon." Nicole stressed that she can enjoy food and lead a fulfilling life, as long as she balances it with physical activity. As a plus-size model, she does not have to deny herself this basic pleasure of life, as is commonly the case in straight-size modeling.

After a fashion show, I followed a group of plus-size models to the kitchen prep area where they helped themselves to a platter of leftover sandwiches and brownies. While piling a second sandwich onto her plate, size eighteen commercial print and runway model Anna appeared conflicted, "I need to watch what I eat." To which Jackie, size sixteen showroom and runway model, quipped, "Yeah, I watch what I eat . . . as it goes in!" Beneath the levity of this exchange was an earnest call for self-discipline. Anna recognized that she needed to negotiate her hunger with the physical requirements of modeling. She realized that, at a size eighteen and already at the end of the marketable range for plus-size models, an increase in size would lead to a steep decline in work opportunities.

Complicating this management of model physical capital, several of the models revealed past disordered eating patterns (such as binge eating, compulsive exercising, or yo-yo dieting). Mary, for example, a size fourteen fit model, spent most of her adolescence loathing her body and tried dieting to correct this "defect":

> I even tried this crazy liquid diet and wore little acupressure balls behind my ears. All I ate was a liter of milk and mushy cabbage. After a month, I only lost twelve pounds, and I had to stop because I was too weak to even move.

Having such a strained relationship with food and her body, Mary needed to strike a balance between managing her body and controlling it via excessive means. This required Mary to focus on long-term solutions to body management, e.g., a portion-controlled diet and workout regimen of cardiovascular exercise, like Zumba workouts, and weight training. Mary began eating organic fruits and vegetables, switched to a mostly vegetarian diet with some lean chicken and fish added for protein, and eliminated alcohol from her diet:

> I try to eat healthy, cook simple, easy meals for me and my boyfriend. I'm conscious of calories, but I'm not hyper-vigilant about it anymore. I made long-term changes because I care about myself and my body. If I didn't, it would show and I wouldn't book any jobs.

Similarly, Anna and Janice, both recovered binge eaters and compulsive exercisers, made long-term, sustainable adjustments. In order to continue to cultivate her body and remain competitive, Anna made minor shifts in her lifestyle:

> I stopped drinking soda. It was so hard. I was addicted. I drink tons of water, now. I always carry a bottle with me. I heard it helps my skin. But, sometimes I'll sneak in a can of Diet Coke.

After eliminating soda from her diet, Anna noticed positive changes to her body and energy level. Switching to water helped even out her complexion. On the other hand, Janice found that the natural pace of living in Manhattan facilitated a sufficient level of bodily management. "I do not go to the gym," she confidently stated. "Never again. I walk everywhere, take the subway, [and] live in a fifth floor walkup [apartment]."

These models managed their physical capital daily, from making minor adjustments in lifestyle to investing in more intensive body projects involving dermatological and orthodontic treatments. Some had to binge and overeat to increase their size. Samantha confessed that on more than one occasion she had purposefully ingested salty foods the night before a meeting with a client in order to retain water and be the correct, slightly larger size for a fitting.

Unlike athletes who have coaches to monitor their progress, these models labored over their bodies alone. They became their own coaches and cheerleaders. Their bodies were both subject and object, mindfully managed through self-monitoring and discipline. For these plus-size models, they were their bodies and their bodies were their careers.

As we see from this aesthetic labor process, these women went from "doing looks" to "doing plus size." Working within an institution that places a high economic value on the physical body, these models wage a personal battle to control and discipline their bodies. This pressure intensified for those women who work as fit models.

Fit Models

During an ordinary research-oriented evening sitting in front of my computer and perusing a stack of articles from *Women's Wear Daily* (a fashion-industry trade journal), I received a call from an agent at the modeling agency with which I was signed. The agent informed me that there was a new "fit" client who wanted to see me. "Great," I hastily replied, until the agent continued, "for lingerie and swimwear." Up until that point, I had modeled casual and evening attire. The thought of parading in underwear for a couple of strangers while being poked, prodded, and pinned roused all of my bodily insecurities. In lingerie or swimwear, you cannot hide, securely nestled within a pair of control top pantyhose or Spanx. The flesh is on full display, and, depending on the style and cut of said garment, my body—flaws and all—would be visible.

I could not decline the casting, lest I forgo my relationship with the agency. So, for the next few days before the scheduled meeting, I resumed my lapsed Pilates and cardio routine and fasted with a detoxifying cranberry concoction. I prepped both my body for its possible full disclosure and my self-conscious mind for humiliation and, what I feared most, the client's revelation that I was absolutely clueless about fashion design.

The day of the fit casting, I headed to the specified address in midtown Manhattan, where I was buzzed inside a design factory showroom. A drone emanating from the rows of active sewing machines accompanied my stroll to the back, where I was handed a pair of pajamas and asked to change behind a screen. The client then measured me, took snapshots from the front, side, and back, and asked me questions about the feel and fit of the pajamas. I was then asked to try on a nightgown, as she explained that these were items from a new line aimed at mature women, designed for a private label brand of a leading discount department store. Within a span of ten minutes, the casting was done and I had dodged a scantily clad bullet.

Fashion designers and clothing manufacturers hire fit models to try on garments at various stages of production to determine the fit and appearance of the garment on a live person. Thus, a fit model's job is to comment on the material and the cut of the garment with respect to its fit and feel as she moves about the way the customer would in the future. The model gives this feedback to the designer before the garment is mass-produced. As one agent described to me, "The fit model is the designer's muse." Fit modeling jobs are billed hourly, with New York City rates ranging from $125 up to $300 per hour, and designers prefer to use the same model throughout a design season; hence, the hours can add up to profitable work. For example, one fit model in my sample earned on average $27,000 a year from fit clients alone. In addition, fit work may potentially lead to print work for the client.

It is essential to this process for the model's measurements to remain constant in order to ensure a consistency of sizing and fit in garment production.[11] As a fit model warned, "If she [the model] is bloated and they [the designers] fit the garment larger, women [in the stores] will think they lost weight." In other words, a designer's usual size fourteen pant may feel roomier than last season's version to the average consumer. While based on a form, the true fit and size of a garment are dependent on the fit model used during fittings. Therefore, the model needs to maintain specific dimensions and proportions, often to within an inch of those she had when she started working for the client.

A fit model is not hired for her perfect body but, rather, for her consistent body. So, throughout the process, clients record and track every inch of a model's body. Changes in her dimensions and proportions could mean lost jobs. Clients fired models whose weight fluctuated. Sarah, a size fourteen/sixteen model, explained to me that she had a recurring working relationship with one designer until she lost ten pounds:

> I was diagnosed with Celiac disease and couldn't eat bread anymore, so I lost weight because I couldn't eat the major food group of my diet. The client was not too happy with my weight loss and fired me. I don't know what I was more pissed at—losing a client or losing bread.

Those ten pounds meant the end of her steady work opportunity.

For some models, this amplified pressure to maintain one's exact measurements in fit modeling countered the financial benefits. Holly, a size sixteen model, refused to work fit jobs because of her history with an eating disorder. She explained, "I know I can make some good money but the last thing that I'm gonna do is worry like that. I can keep this [body] in check but I'm not gonna worry about every pound." Holly successfully disciplined her body so that she maintained her size in order to work in commercial print and runway, but she feared that the added strain of working as a fit model would trigger an eating disorder relapse.

The Shame of Losing Weight

What happens if a model fails to maintain her weight? The case of fit model Janice offers a telling tale of what can happen when a plus-size model loses weight. When I spoke to Janice, she had recently lost weight as an unintended consequence from an attempt at bodily improvement. She invested in a retainer to straighten her teeth; however, it was not until after the retainer was made that the doctor instructed her that she would have to wear it for twenty-three hours a day. In order to eat, she would have to remove it and then brush her teeth before she put it back on. As a result of the inconvenience this orthodontic treatment caused, Janice lost twenty pounds in a matter of weeks.

When Janice went to her fitting jobs, she noticed a marked difference in the reactions of the clients who disapproved of her weight loss. A designer client, who hired Janice to fit dresses, sweaters, and shirts for the past three years, stood in horror and exclaimed, "I am going to have to measure you. You lost weight."

To Janice's own amazement, she had lost three inches in her waist and four inches in her bust and hips. The client then replaced Janice with some other "big girl." Because of this dramatic weight loss, Janice no longer fit the position as fit model and lost about $5,000 a year from this one fit client alone. Having lost the weight and a well-regarded job opportunity, Janice experienced a shame equivalent to that one feels after gaining weight. Confused, she confided, "I hate being told it [the weight loss] is wrong. It is my body."

At another job doing line work for a nationwide retailer, where fit models of various sizes literally line up to model the latest design collection for corporate directors, Janice tried on her usual size eighteen pant, but after buttoning the waist, the pants fell to the floor. She was immediately given a smaller size pant:

> I felt like I was being arrested. The looks I got from these people. I started
> to give a monologue to the directors, saying I had just had food poisoning
> and made cracks about eating muffins to gain the weight back.

Conflicted by the demand from her clients that she needed to gain back at least ten pounds and worry about paying bills, Janice broke down under the pressure and bought weight gaining powder.

In an industry where the body is a commodified object, a model may sometimes need to engage in deviant behaviors to remain marketable. As in the aforementioned case, when fit clients fired Janice because she lost too much weight, she returned to the binge mentality she learned years ago while in college, where she would binge on carbohydrates and cheese and then exercise the next day. This time, however, she did not exercise the next day but, instead, "walked slow" and carried a jar of peanut butter in her bag, consuming it by the spoonful. Janice suffered flashbacks from that previous episode in her life and could no longer stomach her daily Ensure shakes mixed with strawberries and ice cream.

As a newly slimmed down plus-size model, Janice experienced resistance from fit clients, who demanded that she return to her larger size. Janice struggled with the issue of having to gain weight in an unhealthy manner, something she never thought she would have to do as a plus-size model. Here, the fit clients demanded a specific body that Janice could not provide.

This push toward fatness and gaining weight is counter to what contemporary American culture dictates about women's bodies. While fashion urges everyday women to lose weight, fashion urges plus-size models, at times, to gain weight. One model admitted that her agent took her out to dinner and encouraged her to eat in order to gain a size. Models push their bodies to extremes. Fashion allows these women to be fat, and, sometimes, urges them to get fatter in order to build their model physical capital.

Who's the Beauty Boss?

In the fall of 2011, TLC premiered a reality program called *Big Sexy* that featured five self-identified plus-size women who worked in the fashion industry as models, stylists, and makeup artists. Their mission was to challenge contemporary bodily aesthetics that privileged the thin body and equate fat with sex appeal. In an interview for *The Huffington Post*, one of the featured women, Heather, explained, "You can be whatever size you want to be and work in the fashion industry."[12] However, in the first episode of the program, the audience learned that her statement was an exaggeration as we watched another cast member, Tiffany, meet with her modeling agent. In the exchange, the agent informed Tiffany that a client wanted her to lose weight and that "it's a waste of time and money if the numbers are not right." Tiffany's measurements had increased since the agent last took her measurements, and Tiffany would need to lose between seven and ten pounds to meet the client's size expectations. At her present size, Tiffany was dangerously close to exceeding the boundaries of plus size required of models.

Modeling agents were responsible for advising their models on how to present themselves to prospective clients—what to wear to castings, what to say to clients. In exchange for offering their models access to castings and clients, agents expected full disclosure and compliance from them. Models and their agents engaged in an intimate working relationship, where even private matters of the body were subject to public scrutiny. Individual body projects, such as simply changing a hair style and color or something more extreme such as getting a tattoo or body piercing, were negotiated and evaluated together with the agent based on issues of fashion trends and employment potential. Agents determined the final look of their models. Agents, not the models themselves, had the final say.

I quickly learned that, as a model, I lost agency over my own body during my first meeting with Bobby. After he offered to send me out to castings, Bobby quickly advised me to "keep clean" Sunday night through the workweek till Friday. He warned, "I don't care what you do on your weekends but be sober and not bloated for Monday morning. You will not know too much in advance when you will have a casting, so be prepared." This was the standard advice he offered to all his models, which served to set control parameters on his models' behaviors. Even on my personal time, I was subject to Bobby's gaze.

Bobby then continued with his spiel on work ethic and ground rules for his agent-model relationship. For example, I was directed to never alter my body or hair without first consulting him. I was to seek his consultation if I wanted to try a new hairstyle. In fact, Bobby specifically warned me to never color my hair. For added emphasis, he recounted the story of one model who he referred to as a plus-size version of Nicole Kidman with luscious red hair, who vacationed in Europe and, on a whim, bleached her hair blonde. "It was poorly done," Bobby lamented, as he recalled having to call and explain to casting directors why the promised redheaded bombshell was now a bleached blonde. As a consequence, the model lost work due to the lack of her signature hair color, and Bobby lost his share of the commission. In addition, his working relationship with these casting directors soured. According to Bobby, the model made the mistake of making both him and the agency look unprofessional. This model failed to abide by Bobby's rules. She decided, without his consent, to change her look.

From Alex and her use of padding to Janice and her quick weight gain binge, these plus-size models labored over their bodies to appeal to their agents and potential clients. These plus-size models became products that clients fixed up and dressed up to present as desirable packages. Agents sold these manufactured packages to clients, who in turn resold them to consumers. These models were interchangeable bodies with dyeable hair and fixable features.

As "docile" bodies, they engaged in constant battle to control and discipline their bodies. They developed a repertoire of specialized professional techniques to increase their "model physical capital." Technologies of control, such as a tape measure, legitimized and normalized this constant surveillance of the body. As part of the physical strategies employed by plus-size models to remain marketable to clients, models tracked each measurement and manipulated their bodies by either invasive or non-invasive techniques, ranging from strict dieting and exercise to wearing padding in the appropriate places.

Beauty is a social construction, but these women were not the ones in charge of its construction. Plus-size models must conform to an image created by fashion's tastemakers—agents and designers. Their bodies need to fit within narrowly defined parameters, often within a fraction of an inch. Ultimately, they mold their bodies to fit an image, instead of being empowered in a way that allows them to mold the image to fit their bodies. These women were not challenging a contemporary definition of beauty. They were changing their bodies into shapes and sizes that were predetermined by others to be acceptable.

5

Agents as Gatekeepers of Fashion

When my proofs from the test shoot arrived, I was eager to choose which shots would be printed for my modeling portfolio and composite card. Originally, Bobby expressed his plan for choosing the images on his own; however, I was eager to see the results of my long day of posing and dressing up and insisted that I join him. I wanted my voice to be heard in the deliberations.

Upon viewing the images through a photographer's loop, I marveled at the results. As Bobby summarized, I photographed well—I successfully engaged in affective labor during the shoot and it came across in the proofs—though problematically thinner than my actual size ten frame, which appeared more like a size six or eight body on film. I secretly reveled in the news, my merriment only dampened by the fact that I was in the office of the director of a *plus-size* agency.

Bobby described the last look from the shoot as the plus-size "money shot," which highlighted "the bum, boobs, and arms." In my personal opinion, I thought that particular image was unflattering precisely because it emphasized my "bum, boobs, and arms." I secretly wished a warning could appear with the image, "Objects in this photo are smaller than they appear." I argued with Bobby over his selection of that particular image, but he reasoned:

I picked this one [he points to one image in the biker series] because it shows off your body and the angle of your cheekbones. Your eyes are

beautiful . . . You look like a plus-sized girl here. Look, in this one [point-
ing to the proof page from look three] *you don't*, you really don't. You
really don't shoot plus-size at all. You look really skinny here—no curves.
Here, you don't have any form. No one can get a really good look unless
you do another shot with, like, something that is body. There is no body
here. The client needs to see what the body looks like. Get it?

I understood the rationale underlying his analysis of the film and agreed
with the need to display the body, but I hesitated to finalize the selec-
tions. My image was immortalized in those photographs. Those images
represented me. I wanted to protect *my* image, especially since I felt it was
not satisfactorily depicted. I equated thinness with good looks and, from
the entertainment industry perspective, good work. After countless years
trying to look thinner for my acting career, I would not permit any wide
angles or stray rolls of skin to be visible in the photographs. I wondered,
too, how much of the "excess" could be retouched.

This clashed with my personal preconceptions of beauty, derived from
a cultural perspective where thinness equates with desirability, and professional expectations of plus-size models to display what Bobby referred
to as "the bum, boobs, and arms." Instinctively, I wanted to cover my
arms and suck in my stomach. Rather, a plus-size model displays those
exact parts, areas of the body that the popular cultural discourse maligns
and subjects to modification. New to the industry, I had not fully fath-
omed the personal implications of putting my body on display nor the
demands these fashion tastemakers would require of me.

Stubborn, I continued to debate Bobby on the merits of that singular
image. Ultimately, he gave me a choice:

None of these are bad. The photographer did their job. If I thought it was
terrible, I would say "Oh, my god, please re-shoot it." I think that these are
really nice for a first shoot. You are lucky that you got so many good shots.
Some people have less to choose from than this. Sometimes people come
back with terrible pictures and I go, well, I can't work with you . . . If you

don't like it then certainly by no means print it. It's up to you whether you want to blow it up [to enlarge the image to a 9x12 print] or not. It's your money. But, um, if you are going to spend money on your card, I would say you are going to need at least another body shot. There is no body here. If you want to shoot again or test with someone else, fabulous. It's totally your call. We are not here to not serve you.

If I intended to make a genuine effort at modeling, I needed to curb my bodily anxiety. I needed to work *with* Bobby, form a partnership between fresh model and knowledgeable agent. By the conclusion of the meeting, we agreed on three images, compromised on the fourth, and organized the layout of the composite card.

Shifting from the aesthetic labor of a plus-size model, in this chapter I focus on the gateway to the production of beauty—the modeling agency. I examine the work agents do and their relationship with their models. Agents develop a paternalistic management style with their models, in which these models become subordinate and subject to specialized management tools and practices that coordinate the modeling work processes. A prime example of this is the "booking board," which serves as the tangible nexus of power in an agency. A booking board is a pictorial roster of signed plus-size models, a physical catalog of the collective body capital of an agency. Agents take great pride in their board and continually work to improve its overall image by manipulating the images, themselves, as well as the models depicted in them. I conclude with an examination of the consequences of a paternalistic management style, when an agent's involvement in his or her model's life ventures beyond professional matters. Individual body projects are no longer private but, rather, group efforts. The aesthetic labor models undergo requires them to self-surveil their bodies on a daily basis; their agents, as referees, ensure they are keeping up with the demands of the job. Agents evaluate, critique, and motive their models. Sometimes, this mentorship can cross the line from acceptable and necessary to unwarranted and destructive.

A Model's Guide

All the novelty of the fashion industry may overwhelm the fledgling fashion model. Factor in dreams spun from designer threads and hopes captured in a Times Square billboard, a woman may easily get lost amid the hoards of other doe-eyed wannabees. The field of fashion has its own rules, rules that are in constant flux with the shift in seasons. One day, you are "in," and the next you are "out." *Auf Wiedersehen*, as supermodel Heidi Klum would say.

As one of these aspirants, I walked into open modeling calls unsure of the appropriateness of my dress, shoes, and degree of makeup application while being surrounded by a clique of boisterous plus-size models who enjoyed flaunting their size and shape in front of one another like proud peacocks. They had confidence in their bodies and their work. They all seemed to know each other. I, on the other hand, felt unknown and alone. I did not know how to present myself as a model. I lacked style. I did not know the standard operating procedures or the jargon.

As an actor, I had a manager, agents, and an acting coach help me navigate the whole process. They guided me through each step, from how to greet the casting directors to how to look and act like a scripted character. For auditions, I wore a specific outfit meant to convey the "girl-next-door" persona. At auditions, I studied the "sides," i.e., script of a short scene to perform in front of the casting directors. All the actors quietly prepared before being called into the audition room. An apprehensive silence, broken by the occasional faint mutterings of actors rehearsing their lines, filled the halls. Few actors interacted with each other, since we were all busy preparing ourselves and "getting into character." This was in sharp contrast to the rambunctious party atmosphere of plus-size modeling castings. Without a script to study, models simply had more time to chitchat before casting called them into the casting room to perform. Socializing became their way of stimulating their energy reserves and engaging in affective labor. It also served as a means of gathering information on additional job opportunities.

Similar to my acting management team, models have an equivalent support system. For many plus-size models, their help comes in the form of a modeling agent. Agents across the various performance careers perform similar tasks. As in body performance-centric fields such as boxing, dance, and modeling, social actors (here, the models themselves) "create and mold their bodies in accordance with the fields in which they are involved and the demands of those specific fields."[1] In the field of modeling, these plus-size models are classified and molded by the institutional habitus of the fashion industry, where agents play a central role in preparing women to be models by instilling in them a particular mind-set.[2] These women not only engage in aesthetic labor to physically alter their bodies to meet the demands of the profession; they also alter their self—their feelings and dispositions—according to fashion's tastes. Transforming a "fat woman" into a "plus-size model" takes a team of aesthetic professionals. Both models and agents engage in work practices that are focused on harnessing aesthetic labor and developing marketable bodies.

As described in chapter 4, a model prepares her body for the performance of modeling. Her job is to use her body to strike the right pose and "sell a garment" for the client. In order to effectively do so, a model regulates and disciplines her body. By way of toning and shaping her body through diet and exercise or artificial enhancements, the model prepares her body for the changing needs of clients. As freelance workers, models continue to modify their physical capital amid fluctuating conditions in the fashion market, as their agents guide and approve their actions.

While plus-size models self-monitor and train to increase their model physical capital, their agents network with fashion clients on behalf of the models. They negotiate the market's demand for models and evaluate their models' potential. Agents within a modeling agency cooperate to develop their talent, investing time and money. Specifically, modeling agents represent models, working to prepare and develop these women for the fashion industry, i.e., guide them through the initial steps of building a modeling portfolio. As talent scouts, modeling agents serve to find and produce marketable models. They meet with their models in the agency office or email them, provide details on bookings and castings, discuss career options, or check-in on the condition of their bodies. For example, one agent cheerfully described her division as "a family-oriented board. We are constantly advising our models and discuss among ourselves [the agents] what direction to take each of them."

This hands-on approach takes time and energy. In agencies with upwards of forty-something plus-size models, it would be impossible for an agent to contact each model daily while also dealing with clients, so, like in every family, there are favorites. The level of instruction differs depending on each model's stage of career development. For new models "fresh off the boat," agents will take a more hands-on approach to develop the woman into their image of a model. The agency will direct the fledgling model to a photographer for test shots, confer with hair stylists for the appropriate color and cut, and shop with her to find outfits to be worn for castings.

Agents assume a paternalistic management style, guiding new models through the process of starting a career in modeling. The agent will walk a new model through the initial steps of the business by training her how to walk and pose, sending her for test shots, organizing her portfolio, and putting together her composite card. Often, these agents affectionately refer to their models as "my girls," highlighting the personal and possessive dimensions of the job as agent.

On the other hand, for established models who are either switching agency representation or have been working at the local level for some time, agents, in practice, tend to limit their contact with them to simple scheduling matters. As an agent confessed, "If a product works, why change it?" This candid revelation, where the agent equates the model with a product, speaks of the commodification of the model's body and the role the agent plays in preparing it for "production." In these cases where models continue to book work, agents allow the process to run without much interference.

Evaluating Market Potential Costs Money

The organizational structure of the modeling industry, built on the production and distribution of cultural items, relies on the work of agents acting as "gatekeepers." This structure delineates the responsibility of discovering and sponsoring new models into the field to agents. Much of this work of scouting for new talent is done on the street. Scouting is a continuous process where agents do not always wait for models to come to them. They look for prospective models (of all sizes and types) while walking down city streets or riding on public transportation. For seasoned agents, it only takes a few seconds to evaluate a woman's potential—her affective labor. While speaking with the director of a plus-size division, the agent informed me that she had an appointment with a potential model later that afternoon whom she first noticed while looking out of her office window. "I looked out [of my window] and saw a beautiful woman," she recalled. "I sent my assistant after her to get her in." For agents, scouting is an instinctual skill, cultivated over time. Some find it difficult to "turn off the eye" for scouting, even while vacationing. Another agent regretted the time he refrained from approaching a young girl while vacationing in South America. He was convinced she could have been a star with some training.

As sociologist (and former fashion model) Ashley Mears explained in *Pricing Beauty: The Making of a Fashion Model*, which focused on straight-size models, fashion professionals subject models to uncertain judging criteria:

> Their key task [as agents and bookers] is to keep track of the field of fashion producers, to predict and produce the tastes of their clients, and to fit the right kind of bodily capital into the right opening at just the right moment . . . Bookers face an especially tough predicament, given the inherent uncertainty involved in selling something as ephemeral as a look.[3]

Plus-size models, too, are susceptible to this uncertainty and are at the mercy of an agent and his or her willingness to try to sell her look. Velvet D'Amour experienced this firsthand when she took her chances at a top New York City modeling agency after losing eighty pounds as a result of taking Fen-phen:

> I remember going in and she looked at my pictures and she said, "You know, your nose is too wide. Your chin is too long. And your eyes are too close together." It was very, very berserk. Here I had lost all this weight and I was thinking, "woo hoo," and thought I looked really great.

This agent had a well-defined concept of a marketable model that Velvet could not match; yet, Velvet received more than a simple rejection. She gained insight into a beauty ethic espoused by the fashion industry that is not always consistent. One hopeful plus-size model may be turned away by one agency and signed by another the next day. Body aesthetics change. Agents, as gatekeepers within a cultural industry, navigate through a fluctuating market demand for models.

What these cases demonstrate is that the modeling industry has strict yet unpredictable standards of what is considered marketable. While proportionality of body and facial features is required from any model despite prevailing trends, a desirable look can vary from season to season because clients "shape taste and inculcate new consumerist dispositions rather than respond passively to consumer demands."[4] It is the role of the agent, as mentor and job hunter, to assess trends in fashion and guide his or her models through this uncertainty. It is the agent who advises the model on how to dress for a particular client and what to say to land the job.

Beyond possessing a desirable (i.e., marketable) look, a model needs to know how to sell that look through posing. To evaluate a model's posing aptitude, an agent first sends her to a photographer for a test shoot. A test shoot evaluates a model's capacity for affective labor, i.e., her ability to emote well for the camera. These shoots are also an opportunity for the model to test her skills and figure out which poses flatter her body. One agent equated this test shoot with entering a trade school to learn a craft. According to the agent, "This first step [the test shoot] is Modeling 101. The next step is Modeling 102, learning to smile and work with the arms." A model can learn how to effectively pose from testing in front of a camera and later surveying the proofs. As one model mentioned, she studied her proofs to learn how to pose for the camera:

> I analyze each shot on the CD to nitpick and improve on what I'm doing. Clients want the shot, so I need to deliver within a few shots. They're not going to wait around all day for me to get into the zone.

By carefully examining each frame, she learned the most effective way to perform for the camera. Her goal was not only proficiency but also efficiency. This testing process is ongoing; it is not without cost.

The startup costs of modeling can be a heavy burden for a model, as photographer's fees and prints resulting from a single mandatory test shoot can cost anywhere from a few hundred to a few thousand dollars, depending on the photographer and the number of looks to be photographed. These test shots, along with composite cards, at the bare minimum, are required as the model's basic marketing tools, but some models may also attend modeling workshops and classes, schedule regular salon appointments to maintain a camera-ready appearance, and invest in tailored garments. All of these preparatory expenses add up. These sunk costs do not guarantee future modeling work but are necessary to compete in the business.

While a single test shoot is not ideal, an agent may be sensitive to a model's financial situation, as Bobby had been in preparing me for the economic reality of modeling:

> You see, for every new model we work with, we would like to have them shoot four or five times. Realistically, who has that kind of money? I mean, unless, you are a countess or something or you have friends who

are photographers who can work a shot. It's a process. After you make some money, I would test again.

As stated earlier, building a model's book is a process that involves capturing a variety of marketable looks that clearly display the model's physical appearance and demonstrate her ability to convey personality on film. These looks can range from high-fashion editorial to commercial and catalog.

As fashion styles change, a model's portfolio may need updating, as well. At the request of her agency, Clarissa, a size fourteen commercial print model, needed to update her book. After a decade of appearing in catalogs and promotional campaigns for both domestic and European retail outlets, her agency decided that she needed edgier, more high-fashion looks in her portfolio. Although she was a commercial success, Clarissa's agency wanted her to widen her appeal to a market that was shifting to a younger, edgier look. So, even she, with a book full of tear sheets—a page cut from a magazine or catalog to prove the publication of an image—from dozens of ad campaigns, had to reshoot and overhaul her modeling image to remain current.

Even my agent made a similar recommendation: "You look young. Once you work a bit and need to reinvest, I will send you to someone else [a photographer] and go younger in the looks." Unlike Clarissa, I had the opposite issue with my book. My original test shoot produced looks that were on the edgier side, so my second agency recommended I test again for more commercial looks. Since a model's book is her resume, a diversity of looks helps to appeal to a greater number of clients and maintain employability despite fluctuating market demands. Above all, marketable youth and beauty are the goal of any look in a model's book.

Some agencies, like full-service agencies that manage multiple divisions, will front the initial costs of a test shoot with an in-house photographer, printing fees for prints and composite cards, salon appointments for hair cut and style, and a suitable wardrobe for the beginning model. Later, they deduct these costs from a model's subsequent earnings. This system can save a model from the initial financial burden; however, it also leaves models indebted to the agency until these "loans" are repaid.[5] Models have gone into debt, despite a steady work schedule, because their agency appropriated most of their earnings to cover agency fees charged to their account. After all of these expenses and deductions, models make far less than expected. Consequently, any work becomes good work, as models cannot afford to be choosy in the types of job opportunities they accept. This leaves them vulnerable and dependent on their agency.

In smaller, boutique agencies, agents refer models to select photographers and stylists for their test shoots. The models, themselves, pay the expenses of the photography sessions, including the hair and makeup artists and the additional costs associated with retouching and printing the enlargements and composite cards. The agencies establish relationships with these aesthetic professionals and rely upon them to provide feedback about the model's behavior and modeling potential while on set for the test shoot. These evaluations weigh in agencies' general assessment of a model. If an agency decides not to enter into a contractual agreement with a model, she may use the photos from the test shoot with another agency but that agency may want something else, like the agent who wanted to see more commercial shots of me. For a model just starting out, retesting may be too much of an initial financial hurdle. With the high start-up cost and continual self-investment in the body, most models can only hope to break even in the end.

To Sign or Not to Sign

Is it necessary for a plus-size model to sign with an agency? Many of the plus-size models that I met during my fieldwork hopped from one open casting call to the next in search of work without being represented by an agency. Several freelanced with an agency or two, i.e., an agency agreed to send them out to castings without signing an exclusive contract but collected a commission from any booked jobs through them. Models without agency representation trudge through what one agent described as "the underground modeling market" alone and often unprepared.

Marilyn, who as a teen started her fashion career as a straight-size model and transitioned to commercial print, runway, and fit modeling as a size fourteen/sixteen model, offered advice on how to navigate this "underground modeling market":

> If you are looking for a fun and interesting hobby, then by all means shoot with anyone you can [a photographer or client] and have a great time. You can submit to casting calls online. They are often posted on Craigslist. But realize that often these jobs may only be to trade for photos or occasionally clothing. Often the jobs that pay or the clients with jobs that pay go through agents. I have worked for some smaller startup companies that initially paid me very little, but as they grew, they used me again and paid me more. So you never know.

As Marilyn explained, work generated without the use of an agency is usually not paid work. Instead, a client offers the model prints from the shoot or clothes from the show in exchange for her services. Amateur photographers will often do this in hopes of capturing good-quality images that serve to bolster their own portfolios. Designers and boutiques use models in showrooms aimed at fashion buyers for large department stores. Runway shows are unpaid but provide exposure for models. From working for free or in exchange for goods to being required to sell tickets to fashion shows, beginning models comply in order to gain experience and add prints to their portfolios.

Unsigned models learn to navigate the local and regional levels of the modeling market without the aid of an agency. This can become tedious, as they need to scour multiple Internet sources to find modeling opportunities. As Marilyn stated, these models resort to websites like Craigslist and Facebook, online forums dedicated to plus-size modeling, and listservs to find information about castings. This can be risky, as the fashion field is rife with those who prey on naïve, uninformed models.

Without an agency to legitimize a casting, a model may fall victim to a scam. Most scams typically involve high-pressure sales pitches for modeling classes and photo shoots that can range in price from several hundred to several thousand dollars. A tell-tale sign of a scam is an "agent" who charges a model an up-front fee to serve as her agent. The unregulated nature of this "underground modeling market" means that anyone can post a notice for a casting, leaving unsuspecting models vulnerable to those with nefarious purposes.

These worst-case scenarios aside, a model can still find legitimate and profitable work without an agency. After Janice lost her fit clients because of her dramatic weight loss, she surreptitiously managed to get the contact information for several intimate apparel companies from a former client. She brazenly contacted the clients directly in search of work opportunities, successfully booking a few jobs. Unsigned models rely upon informal social networks to gain access to work opportunities. Consequently, they tend to band together, creating their own community of support and information sharing.

For those without agency representation, former models and runway coaches serve as mentors. Several of the models shared a mentor named Carol—a veteran plus-size model who worked as an image consultant. As someone with more than twenty years in fashion, she was their "fashion godmother," arranging meetings with agents and using them in her various projects from runway events to on-air fashion demonstrations for morning news television programs without charging a commission for her services.

While these kinds of social resources can aid a model's quest, working with an agency is a model's best route for advancing a career in fashion because agencies provide models with a larger and more prestigious client pool. For example, Lane Bryant primarily hires models who are represented by either the Ford or Wilhelmina modeling agencies. Agents are at the heart of a field of cultural production that consists of a network of models and clients. Potential models, like Caroline from chapter 4, seek out agent representation to increase their network connections.

Part of an agent's job is to develop relationships with designers, photographers, advertising agencies, and related fashion professionals. Agents connect models to potential clients. For example, if a fashion designer needs a model for an upcoming advertising campaign, agents will present their models for consideration and make a case for them to the designer.

Agents develop and commodify embodied actors, similarly seen in Deborah Dean's study of stage and screen actors in her book, *Performing Ourselves: Actors, Social Stratification and Work*.[6] Dean found that perception guides the casting process. Typically, casting directors send agents a brief and usually vague description of a character. Then, the agents select which actors, in their opinions, suit the character and direct them to the audition. Agents influence the casting process by offering their choice in performers and negotiating with casting behind the scenes. In modeling, agents similarly seek and proceed to "talk up" their models to clients. They paint an attractive and profitable image of their girls by selling their corporal strengths. Ultimately, agents receive a commission based on this verbal transaction. Agents not only develop the embodied attributes of their models, they package them to clients in an appealing narrative.

While it is possible to find work as an unsigned model, these models usually freelance with an agency or two; such was the case of Marilyn. She explained the benefits of a non-exclusive working relationship:

> I am signed with an agency. They are wonderful to work with, and having an agent certainly helps expose you to clients that have the jobs that pay well. I am non-exclusive, so I am able to freelance, but I have found that since I am represented by an agency I can ask for higher freelance rates than I got beforehand.

Models may also be signed with different agencies in the different modeling markets. For example, one model used one agency for work in New York City, a second in Los Angeles, and a third in Miami.

Being represented by an agency is generally the best course of action, especially if the model is serious about pursuing a career in modeling, because of the hierarchical organization of the profession. Unsigned models working in this "underground market" at the local and regional levels in catalog and boutique showrooms constitute the lowest levels of the hierarchy, followed by models signed to specialized, boutique agencies. Those few models signed to large, international modeling agencies and, thus, more likely to appear in editorials for fashion magazines and on runways in New York City to Milan are at the top of the career ladder. While it is possible for a model to move up the ranks, her career prospects depend on a combination of chance and genetics, in addition to hard work and persistence despite continual rejection.

"Let Me Show You My Board"

Overall, the agent's role is to discover and market the strengths of his or her models. The structure of modeling, like many body-centric fields, is essentially a network of differential relations between social actors that involves both a highly developed canon of body techniques and those social actors who can synthesize these techniques.[7] Focusing on the relationship between plus-size model and agent reveals a discourse of power and control. This is epitomized by the booking board, which is at the heart of the modeling agency.

Comprised of sleek shelving that holds rows of composite cards, this booking board is a tangible nexus of power for the agency, cataloguing the collective body capital of the agency, i.e., its roster of signed plus-size models. This instrument is centrally located within an agency and is continually referred to by the agents as they pick and choose which models to send out to castings.

Agents exude pride when speaking of their board. After an interview with an agent, he or she enthusiastically asked, "You want to see my board?" This pride also translates into how these agents perceive and work on their boards. As one agent described, she continually tweaks the board, focusing on the color palate and the angles used in the photographs, because "it all speaks to my division. It is about the energy of the board, which clients read." The agent personally picks the photographers used to shoot the models, designs the layout of the composite cards for her plus-size models, and chooses the layout, angles, and colors for printed booklet advertisements that the agency sends out quarterly to clients and photographers.

The board represents the agency itself and the kind of models it produces. In a paternalistic manner, agents take ownership of their models and their images. "Their girls" are their creation and their moneymakers. With strict standards of business, agencies demand much from their models because, as every agent insisted, they give one hundred percent to their girls.

Agents do more than manage the logistics. As an agent described, "We look into women's souls. We show them [the models] how beautiful they are. We walk them through a process of awakening. We offer spiritual and emotional self-help." This help can range from the type of critique Bobby offered regarding my test shoots or one that is focused on motivating the model during periods of self-doubt and rejection. Agents encourage their models when they do good work and offer constructive criticism when needed. For example, Bobby offered this motivational piece of advice to beginning models:

> When you go to castings where most of the girls will have full portfolios, you don't have that much in the book. The ones on your comp card will be the only pictures you have. At times, it could get a little frustrating. [But] it only takes one person to believe in you.

Beyond these types of motivational talks, agents demonstrate their confidence in their models by developing a close professional relationship with them.

Agents take their work personally and are protective over their business, expecting loyalty from their models. The agent-model relationship is a partnership built and nurtured over time, which explained one agent's disdain for models who switch agencies. He viewed it as an act of disloyalty to the original agency.

When I first met Bobby, he stressed that he required my full cooperation. He stressed, "Let me know what is up—your schedule and limitations, whether no nudity or not working on high holy days." If we were to work together, I needed to be up-front about my level of comfort with different kinds of jobs, i.e., fit jobs, lingerie and swimwear, etc., because when he sent me to a casting, I needed to be prepared to accept the job. This was a condition that I understood. As a taller than average twelve-year-old, my acting manager would arrange auditions for me, often for the role of high school teenager. Many of the parts that I auditioned for contained profanity and sexual situations. One audition, in particular, involved the reenactment of a sexual assault. As a child, I was not comfortable with the scene and refused to audition. Afterward, my manager refused to send me out on auditions since she deemed me "unprofessional" and "immature." Therefore, when Bobby said this, I understood the severity of the situation.

In this partnership, agents work closely with their models to build their careers, getting to know them personally and involving themselves in more private aspects of their models' lives, from searching for an apartment after a model's boyfriend dumps her, to helping with mortgage payments, or walking a model down the aisle at her wedding. As one agent argued, this personal connection is necessary for the professional process to work. Without this complete immersion into every aspect of a model's life, he argued, she would not become a star. This agent needed to be aware of everything that could have a possible effect on his model's capacity to work. Given this ideological stance, some agents blur the lines between public and private, as well as between mentorship and control.

In this close mentoring relationship, agents advise their models on how to present themselves to prospective clients. This, at times, involves learning the fine art of deception. Before my first casting for a fit client, my agent advised me to exaggerate the truth of my experience in fit modeling. If asked by the client about my previous fit work, the agent told me to mention that my grandmother was a seamstress and to over-emphasize my past in theater by saying that I had worked as a fit model for costumes. While my grandmother occasionally made me dresses, blouses, and skirts which required multiple fittings, and I had been fit-ted for costumes throughout high school and college for various musi-cal productions, this "experience" had not prepared me for fit modeling work. In recommending me to present myself as a fit model with experi-ence, the agent taught me how to market my particular set of skills and experiences. These kinds of lies run rampant throughout the fashion industry. Models regularly lie about their age, ethnicity, measurements, and level of experience—often at the behest of their agents. In her eth-nography, Mears writes about how her agents instructed her to subtract five years from her age and either stress or ignore her Korean ethnicity to potential clients.[8] The truth of the body used in fashion imagery is inconsequential as long as she can pass as the desired body. In the end, the façade (and not the substance) is all that matters.

Models and agents engage in an intimate working relationship, where private matters of the body are subject to public scrutiny. Individual body projects, such as a simple haircut, become subject to public debate. A model needs to present any desired body modification to her agent, who, in turn, evaluates the proposed change based on fashion trends and employment potential. Any physical changes that affect a model's appearance need to be approved by her agency. She surrenders herself to a collective of aesthetic professionals who makes decisions about her body.

Models are not only subject to an agent's gaze on matters of the look of her body but also on what she does with her body. At my first meet-ing with Bobby, he warned me to refrain from drugs, alcohol, and salt, lest I become bloated for a photo shoot or casting. One of his former models failed to heed this advice. This lucky young woman booked an advertising campaign with a popular American retailing company. On the day of the photo shoot, she did not appear for her call time, which is the meeting time arranged by the client. After several frantic calls from the client to the agency and Bobby to the model, Bobby discovered that the model was too embarrassed to go to work because she had a hickey. Bobby urged her to go anyway, be friendly to the makeup artist, and pray that the shoot was a fall or winter scene involving scarves. Afterward, he dropped her from the agency due to her lack of professionalism:

> She must have been drunk, high, or willing to get a hickey the size of Rhode Island. I won't work with someone who doesn't treat this [model-ing] as a job . . . She made me look bad. I take it personally if it doesn't work or she's not professional.

This incident illustrated that a model's behavior reflects back onto the agency that represents her. At each casting and booking, both the model's and the agency's reputations are in jeopardy. By signing a model, the agent is, in effect, betting on the model's potential to book jobs. The agent, in turn, depends on the model to behave professionally at castings and bookings, namely by showing up promptly and ready to work at the scheduled call time. If a model fails to comply with these expectations, she will be asked to seek representation elsewhere. Modeling is a job, not a right, as Bobby explained during our first meeting:

> From my past experience, I like working with actors. They know how to do the business. Pure models think they are better than everyone else and privileged. Remember, this is a business.

While I told Bobby that I was a sociologist, my educational credentials did not appear to affect his evaluation of me, except that he approved of the flexibility my academic schedule provided. He was more interested in my past as an actor and its similar emphasis on body work and aesthetics. Bobby highlighted the professionalism needed to work in fashion. It is not about being trendy, "cool," or popular. Models do not just stand in a position and look pretty. Modeling, in his view, is work that requires trust in one's agent, dedication to improving one's bodily capital, and fearlessness to do what clients ask.

Building a successful modeling career requires active involvement on the part of a model. Once a model signs with an agency, she needs to maintain a visible presence. As an agent from an exclusively plus-size agency recommended:

> You don't want to fall through the cracks. You need to call or email to check-in with your agent at least once a week, just to see if anything is happening. Most of the time, there won't be anything happening at the moment, but it is good to keep you fresh in your agent's mind. It shows your interest in your career.

Frequent contact with an agent boosts a model's chances of getting sent out to castings. As one model recommended, "Be charming. Remember names. Send thank you cards and gifts. Most importantly, kiss ass!" In order to succeed, these women become entrepreneurs, commodifying their bodies and engaging in emotional labor to sell their product.

Over the Line?

As much as they promote the use of larger bodies in fashion, agents are not goodwill ambassadors for size acceptance. They are business professionals who rely on specialized management tools and practices, e.g., firm contracts, elusive accounting practices, and scheduling controlled by model bookers, to protect their investment. These institutional texts and discourses that coordinate the work processes within modeling agencies serve to connect the macro-level of the modeling industry with the everyday life of the plus-size model. They also serve to control their models' careers. Ultimately, the model is subordinate to the agent.

Agencies control the financial end of modeling work. They negotiate modeling rates with clients, process work vouchers, and schedule a model's bookings and castings. Relying on a commission-based system of service, if the agent does not find the model paid work, the agent likewise does not get paid. In terms of the employer-employee arrangement, models are independent contractors. They are not employees of a modeling agency. Since models are self-employed, they do not receive health insurance or other employment benefits that usually accompany a salaried position. If contractually signed with an agency, the modeling agent becomes the authorized representative of the model and receives a negotiable 15–20 percent commission from the model's earnings for services rendered. Their services include arranging "go-sees" and castings and negotiating terms of compensation with potential clients for the model. In this commission-based scheme, the agent receives a 20 percent cut of the model's fee (the New York modeling market standard) and charges the client—the designer, advertiser, retailer, or other individuals or company that requires the services of a model—an additional 20 percent on top of the negotiated modeling fee. In total, the agent receives 40 percent for being a middleman. One model offered this frank illustration of the role of the agent as a middleman:

> Agents are pimps, the clients are the johns, and models are prostitutes. The clients don't know what they want. They are just a bunch of out of touch higher-ups. Once they have a model, get used to her, they don't want to change her. The models are used by the pimps, I mean the agents, who try to get more money out of her. She's just a commodity. The agent collects 40 percent, for what? It's me [as the model] that makes the connection with the client. [For agents] It's all about the money.

Her categorization of the model-agent relationship, while extreme, does reflect the nature of agency operations. Models are at the mercy of their agents, who are in control of their schedules and their earnings. Agents tell them which casting to go to and then negotiate modeling fees for any booked jobs. The model does not have any say in the matter and must follow her agent's direction. The organizational structure of the agency system is such that models need agents and agents need models; yet, it is the model who is an easily replaceable body.

Agencies may include a number of conditions in their contracts. For example, a contract may require exclusivity from a model, i.e., a model may not work with another agency, whether for all types of modeling jobs or a specific type, e.g., fit or runway. A contract may stipulate that if a model is late to a casting or booking, she is then responsible for covering all the financial damages, such as fees for the photographer, stylist, makeup artist, location, and any financial loss for the agency. Other contracts specify that if a model decides to leave her agency, she must continue to pay the agency their commission rate on future work for clients originally booked though the agency for a specified term after the termination of the contract.

Agencies may also offer contracts to freelance models, provided they share revenue from preexisting clients. This happened to one model who had successfully worked freelance for a number of fit and commercial clients. When she approached a reputable agency, she faced a harsh reality:

> The agent said I was too commercial, meaning not pretty enough. I told him the names of a few of my clients, and he sent me to the fit department. There they measured me, a perfect size eighteen, gave me a contract on the spot, and pushed me out the door . . . When I told them that I would sign with them but would not include my preexisting fit clients in the deal, they stopped returning my calls. They only wanted my clients.

This model spent three years developing a working relationship with these clients, who hired her regularly. Once this agency saw her client list they wanted to reap a financial reward without much effort on their part. Ultimately, the accumulation of modeling revenue can drive an agent to sign a model simply to gain access to additional clients.

When an agent goes beyond his or her professional capacities and ventures into a model's personal matters, problems may emerge. Too much involvement can backfire. While agents assume that a more personal relationship with a model is necessary to advance both of their careers, this arrangement presents a model with dilemmas. Where is the line drawn? Once crossed, how does each party maintain an appropriate level of professionalism? What to do if things go awry?

In this subtle intertwining of personal and professional, lines may blur between acceptable, constructive criticism and that which is unwarranted and destructive. For example, Janice's agent called her at all hours, even in the middle of the night, with new ideas on how to boost Janice's marketability. The agent suggested that Janice pursue a variety of body modifications, from changing her hair color to getting a chin implant. Then, when Janice asked her agent what a client thought of her after a casting, the agent simply replied that the client thought Janice was not "pretty enough." Janice did not appreciate her agent's bluntness.

This kind of model-agent relationship was not what Janice envisioned when she signed the contract. Instead of receiving reasonable, constructive criticism, such as "you need to work on your walk" or "that hair color washes you out," she was encouraged to drastically alter her appearance by way of highly invasive procedures. "If there was so much that needed to be 'fixed,' why would she sign me?" Janice wondered. The agent also failed to respect personal boundaries by calling at all hours of the day to berate Janice. After two years, Janice hired a lawyer to rescind the exclusive modeling contract with the agency. Given her experience, Janice is understandably leery of agents.

Institutional-Level Protections?

A model is an independent contractor and therefore not covered under most federal employment statutes. This leaves a model without much recourse in the face of employment discrimination, wage disputes, or worker's compensation and disability. If a relationship between a model and an agent sours, a model may spend hundreds, perhaps thousands, of dollars to hire a lawyer to break the contract. There is no professional labor union for fashion models that can collectively bargain to negotiate compensation rates and working conditions, prevent exploitation, offer health benefits, or provide other workers' protections.[9]

If there were a modeling union, one model asserted, "Maybe 20-year-old models would not be jumping out of buildings!" This was in reference to the death of Russian *Vogue* cover girl Ruslana Korshunova, who leapt from her ninth-floor apartment in New York in 2008.[10] In the past several years, a significant number of straight-size models (women and men) have committed suicide such that blogger and former straight-size model Jenna Sauers wrote the headline, "Suicidal Models Are Fashion's Worst Trend."[11] The insular environment of this industry that promotes bodily insecurity and disembodiment contributes to this alarming trend. For example, in 2009, Korean runway model Dual Kim hung herself in her Paris apartment. A few weeks prior to her suicide, she wrote in her blog that she was "mad depressed and overworked," and in another entry posted that "the more i [sic] gain the more lonely it is . . . i [sic] know i'm [sic] like a ghost."[12]

While there have not been similar media reports of suicide among plus-size models in the past decade, studies find a positive correlation between increased body weight and suicidal ideation and attempts among adolescent girls; extreme perceptions of body weight appear to be significant risk factors for suicidal behavior.[13] While many of the plus-size models that I met received a boost in their self-confidence from working as a model, some still struggled with the corporal demands placed on them by the industry and the overall cultural stigma of fat. Size fourteen/sixteen runway and showroom model Alice acknowledged the heavy emotional toll she faced while dealing with routine rejection:

> I don't even know why I don't get jobs. They [the clients] don't tell me. Am I too big? Too small? Too edgy? Not commercial enough? I'm lost. This is my passion but I really don't know what to do to stop the rejection. Am I not good enough? I work hard, but sometimes I think I should give up.

While Alice responded to the stresses of the aesthetic labor process by contemplating her professional exit from the fashion industry, plus-size model Tess Munster blogged about the "dark side of modeling" and her suicidal thoughts:

> Modeling, and especially living your life in the public eye, is by far the hardest thing I've ever done. You see a different side to people, a very dark side. People use you to get places, they lie to you, manipulate you, then turn around and "love" you all in a day sometimes. I've lost friends, respect, and countless jobs because of my looks, beliefs, or just plain bad luck. Everyone thinks that they know me, therefore judging every move I make constantly . . . For six months last year (and part of this year) I was suicidal, and thought every day that there was no way I could deal with another day. I didn't really tell anyone because I was embarrassed . . . my life looks so glamorous sometimes, and here I am barely able to get out of bed. Still to this day, I'm told what I "should" look like, how I "should" dress, what I "should" or "shouldn't" be eating . . . basically, how I need to be living my life.[14]

Munster faced an overwhelming pressure to conform to an image of beauty dictated by others. The objectification she experienced as a body in fashion became too much of a burden, and she contemplated suicide in order to avoid the abuse.

As independent contractors, models fend for themselves in an industry that preys on insecurity and naiveté. The field is structured such that a model cannot hope to further her career without an agent, leaving her alone and vulnerable. Ultimately, she is dependent upon her agent and a field built on desire and fantasy. However, there are a number of initiatives in the works to address these labor concerns. For the first time, in 2007, fashion models were allowed to join Equity, a trade union for professional performers and creative practitioners in the United Kingdom.[15] The union, partnering with the Association of Model Agents, the British Fashion Council, and the Greater London Authority, works to improve working conditions and fight against exploitation in the modeling industry. In 2010, Equity established set minimum rates of pay for

London Fashion Week shows that increases depending on the number of seasons that the designer has presented his or her collection. Equity models also developed a ten-point code of conduct, historically signed by British *Vogue* in 2013:

> Models hired by companies signed up to the code of conduct . . . get assurances on hours of work, breaks, food, transport, nudity and semi-nudity, temperature, changing rooms and prompt payment. Plus, models under sixteen years of age will not be used in photo shoots representing adult models.[16]

As members of Equity, models also receive worker's benefits such as legal advice and injury compensation.

These standards established by Equity set a precedent for the kinds of benefits and reforms necessary for models working in the United States and inspired efforts to unionize American models. In 2012, straight-size model Sara Ziff founded The Model Alliance, a not-for-profit labor group for all types of models working in the American fashion industry.[17] According to Susan Scafidi, member of the Model Alliance's Board of Directors and director of the Fashion Law Institute at Fordham Law School:

> The fashion industry needs to reject images of beauty that are created through truly ugly means. Shining a light on those unsavory backstage practices is really going to allow the fashion industry, and the modeling industry, and all of the related industries together to create something more beautiful.[18]

The Model Alliance's goals include:

> Provide a discreet grievance and advice service. Improve labor standards for child models in New York. Promote greater financial transparency and

accountability. Provide access to affordable health care. Draft a code of conduct that sets industry-wide standards for castings, shoots and shows.[19]

Ziff and Scafidi hope to give American models a voice in the fashion industry and continually work to earn the support of the cultural taste-makers—designers, photographers, and agencies—to improve working conditions.

In the next chapter, I look into the creation of this fantasy through the images used in retail marketing campaigns. A reluctance and resistance to accept the plus-size niche plagues the retail clothing market. Designers with "skinny vision" fear an association with plus size and, accordingly, limit their size offerings; however, an increasing crop of retail clothing brands recognize the purchasing power of this underserved population. How do these designers contend with a growing segment of consumers who do not fit the standard mold, whose bodies come in a variety of shapes? Beyond matters of size, consumers demand proper fit and on-trend styles that flatter the curves of a larger body instead of hide them. The frustration over the paucity of clothing options is moving more fat women to enter the field as designers. This provides the unique case where the plus-size design niche is a market molded *for* and *by* its own. These designers aim to challenge hegemonic beauty standards and expose the fat body.

6

Selling the Fat Body

Dove's "Campaign for Real Beauty" caused a stir in the summer of 2005 when it used real women who showed their curves in simple white bras and underwear to introduce its line of firming products. On billboards across the nation, the morning news program circuit, and *The Oprah Winfrey Show*, these women flashed their pearly whites while showing off their rounded bellies and bottoms. Media critics heralded these unaltered and un-retouched images of women ranging from a size four to a size twelve (and not the typical size zero or size two of the fashion model) as a progressive move by the company to appeal to the ordinary woman;[1] yet, others doomed Dove as "the brand for fat girls."[2] Dove's advertisements promoting its new line of firming lotion, cream, and body wash reassured women to "celebrate the curves you were born with," as long as these "real curves" were smooth and dimple-free. While size does not determine your beauty status, according to Dove, firmness, as in "beautifully firm skin," does.

Similar images of confident and exposed plus-size models and "larger" women continue to saturate the media landscape. In an episode of *Grey's Anatomy*, plus-size Sara Ramirez uninhibitedly danced in her underwear. A television ad for Lane Bryant's lingerie line, featuring size sixteen model Ashley Graham, went viral after both the FOX and ABC television networks initially refused to air it due to "excessive cleavage."[3] Even reality television programs, such as TLC's *Big Sexy* and NuvoTv's *Curvy Girls*, featured plus-size models as they worked in the field of fashion.

An advertisement for firming products in Dove's "Campaign for Real Beauty."

How does the display of joyous, sexy, and voluptuous women, along-side fashion editorials where skinny is beautiful, desirable, and devoid of expression, transform aesthetics and commercial clothing markets? Who is *this* fleshy woman in the advertisements and catalogs? With the fashion industry as a site of production and circulation of an ideal-ized woman, how do plus-size-oriented fashion professionals challenge negative images of the fat body? To combat thin privilege and develop plus-size models, these fashion professionals create a new identity for fat women by manipulating the image of a stigma.

One area of the retail clothing market poised to reinvent the image of a fat woman is plus-size intimate apparel. The revitalization of plus-size intimate apparel began in February 1996, when Lane Bryant launched a line of plus-size intimates called Intimates by Venezia in its stores.[4] Positioned to be the "seductive equivalent" of Victoria's Secret's offerings, Lane Bryant revamped plus-size lingerie while focused on functionality and fit, as well. The company's designers produced a line that presented a younger and curvier customer with more options than the traditional offerings of large white underpants, i.e., something her grandmother would wear. Advertised as, "Sexy. Luxurious. Sensual. Pure Magic," and "Practical? No. Sensible? Who Cares. Have to have it? Absolutely," the line promised to enhance the natural curves of a Lane Bryant woman.

Then, in 1997, Lane Bryant produced Cacique-branded lingerie and sold it exclusively in its nationwide stores.[5] In 2006, Lane Bryant expanded Cacique, the brand, into the first exclusively plus-size lingerie store. With the opening of fifty Cacique boutiques in 2006 and an addi-tional three hundred planned, curvy women found undergarments "with pizzazz, color, and unabashed sensuality."[6] Available online (at www.lanebryant.com) and in Cacique boutiques, Cacique offered bras in sizes thirty-six to fifty-six, with cup sizes A through I, and intimates in sizes twelve to thirty-two. Once under the same corporate ownership, Cacique mirrored the marketing tactics of its "little" sister Victoria's Secret, while catering to the consumer that Victoria's Secret neglects.

Resembling the store layout of Victoria's Secret, Cacique built upon basic store design to add elements that catered to a curvy woman, namely extra-large dressing rooms, a "fit salon" manned by trained associates who offer one-on-one assistance in the selection and fitting process, and their famed size sixteen mannequins clothed in the latest lingerie offerings.[7]

Unlike at Victoria's Secret, Cacique's goal was to cater to the curves of a fat woman. The layout of the store allowed larger size bras and panties to be displayed throughout the store, instead of hidden away in a drawer or only available for purchase online as was the norm at other retail stores. Beyond the seemingly standard offering of bras in shades of purple, blue, and chocolate brown, Cacique sold less conventional yet spicier items, such as bras with detachable fake-fur trim and crotchless panties.[8] Cacique prepared to fulfill every curvy woman's sexual fantasy. As the Cacique brand advertised, "What language does your body speak? Sensual, Classique, Physical & Flaunt." Given Lane Bryant's established history in the retail of women's plus-size clothing, Cacique posited itself as the authority in intimate apparel for the curvy woman. Cacique boldly asserted that it was "the brand that knows your curves."

Lane Bryant's foray into intimate apparel influenced a broader commercial trend toward developing plus-size-specific lingerie. Retailers pushed to build inventory, selection, and a bra fit that achieved both comfort and sufficient support. They sought out bra styles in cup sizes up through G, H, I, and J, as well as those with larger cup sizes yet smaller band sizes, possibly explained by the surge in breast augmentation procedures.[9] While the style and fit of lingerie lines such as Cacique improved, ready-to-wear brands have not been as accommodating to the plus-size customer.

Resistance and Reluctance in Retail Fashion

Sales and image guide the business of fashion. While profitable sales entice designers to enter the plus-size market, fears of brand spoilage

The store design and layout of Lane Bryant's lingerie store, Cacique, resembles a Victoria's Secret yet offers amenities for plus-size consumers such as larger mannequins and extra-large dressing rooms.

halt their embrace of "larger" women. Meanwhile, the plus-size clothing market, comprised of a large consumer base, has grown continually since the early twentieth century, when Lena Bryant began making garments geared toward women with figures that were more buxom. A Lithuanian immigrant who immigrated to New York City in 1895, Lena Bryant first sold maternity garments in 1904 in a shop on Fifth Avenue in New York City. After Bryant and her husband, Albert Malsin, conducted a survey of 200,000 women from an insurance company and 4,500 of her customers, she found that women with more buxom figures made up a significant portion of the population. Therefore, Bryant shifted her focus from maternity to larger figures in order to clothe this underserved customer. She incorporated the business, Lane Bryant, on June 12, 1914, with stores opened in Chicago, Detroit, and Brooklyn.[10] Today, as the nation's largest and oldest plus-size retailer, Lane Bryant operates over 800 stores across the country that cater to women size fourteen through size thirty-two and opened a sister chain of lingerie boutiques and outlet stores.[11]

Overall, the plus-size clothing market represents only 14 percent of the $104 billion total revenue in women's apparel; however, in the words of the chief industry analyst of the market research firm the NPD Group Marshal Cohen, "opportunity is brewing."[12] In 2005, the plus-size clothing industry grew by 7 percent compared to the 3.4 percent growth in total sales of women's clothing.[13] Market analysts expect sales to rise to 5.2 percent annually compared to a 2.7 percent increase in overall apparel sales over the next five years.[14] By 2017, market analysts expect plus-size retail to earn $9.7 billion (up from an estimated $7.5 billion in 2012 and $6.6 in 2009).[15]

Beyond the staples of plus-size retailers, such as Lane Bryant, Avenue, and Ashley Stewart, more designers and retailers have noticed the sales potential and jumped onto the plus-size bandwagon. For example, Old Navy, Lands' End, Wal-Mart, T.J. Maxx, Marshalls, Lucky Brand, The Limited, and H&M sell plus-size clothing.[16] Old Navy sells "fashion that fits in sizes 16–30" on their website; Lands' End sells up to size 3X (equivalent to a size twenty-four or twenty-six); and Wal-Mart sells women's clothing up to size 5X (equivalent to size thirty or thirty-two). Other stores, such as Ann Taylor and Banana Republic, increased their size offerings up to size eighteen and size sixteen, respectively, in order to appeal to the plus-size market.[17] Lucky Brand reached out to new customers by launching a plus-size collection featuring trendy items such as skinny jeans and leopard-print cardigans.[18] Young women have more options with Torrid, which targets fashionistas ages fifteen to twenty-nine. Stocked with merchandise in sizes twelve to twenty-six, even the mannequins are plus-size at a size sixteen or eighteen.[19] In 2012, the Kardashian sisters entered the plus-size market with their denim line called Kurves.[20]

Despite evidence of growth in the plus-size clothing market, the design community has resisted dressing "larger" bodies. Angellika, the first plus-size model inducted into the Modeling Hall of Fame, noticed this stagnation in the marketplace:

> The plus-size industry hasn't changed as far as clothing options. We have the same stores like Lane Bryant, The Avenue and Ashley Stewart but no "high-end" clothing like Valentino, Chanel or Armani. It's the same ol' story with Madison Ave. Marketing can't get with the curves of the average woman.[21]

As Angellika observed, many in the design community fear the stigma of plus size.

This backlash against plus size is because, according to David Wolfe, creative director at Doneger Group, a consulting firm dedicated to the fashion industry:

> The fashion business is having a hard time being honest. Fashion has kamikaze tunnel vision about women size six and under, ages eighteen to thirty-four, with perfectly proportioned bodies. The whole thing is predicated on a lie.[22]

In light of this "skinny vision," it is not uncommon for more high-end fashion designers to claim that fat women are "not their market." They fear that these undesirable customers would taint the brand's image and, therefore, scare away their core customer base. For example, the notorious Karl Lagerfeld claimed to design "fashion for slender and slim people."[23] In 2004, Lagerfeld terminated his cooperation with the Swedish clothing retailer, H&M, in part because the retailer produced his clothes in sizes larger than he originally intended.

While Lagerfeld exhibited an extreme case of size snobbery, other designers and retailers acted in more subtle ways to prevent fat women from tarnishing their image. While Chico's, a private branded apparel chain aimed at thirty-five- to fifty-five-year-old women, tried to appease their customers' size insecurities by using a unique sizing system in which, for example, their largest size three is equivalent to a size four-teen/sixteen, the company does not want to be associated with plus size. Jim Frain, Chico's senior vice president of marketing, explained:

> It's a business based on fantasy, on entertainment. Yes, we are dressing real women for real situations. But in marketing images, if we err on the side of overweight models or underweight models, we want to err on the side of underweight . . . We do not want to be mistaken as a plus-size company; that would be very bad. It's a matter of perception versus reality.[24]

According to Marshal Cohen, chief analyst for the market research firm NPD Group, this form of retail prejudice is not surprising since "some brands don't want the image of their product to be associated with a larger-size gal, because it doesn't portray an image of a cool, young, sexy brand."[25] For example, Abercrombie & Fitch (A&F), the brand for the "cool" and "good looking," only sold women's clothing up to a size ten. In a 2006 interview, A&F CEO Mike Jeffries snapped:

> A lot of people don't belong [in our clothes], and they can't belong. Are we exclusionary? Absolutely. Those companies that are in trouble are trying to target everybody: young, old, fat, skinny.[26]

Jeffries apologized for these comments in May 2013, after this interview resurfaced and sparked public outcry over the brand. Spurred by this wave of criticism and declining sales, soon afterward in November 2013, A&F announced that they would expand their sizing options, with larger sizes offered online for some of its women's clothing as early as the spring of 2014, indicating that this exclusionary policy may not have been cost-effective for the company.[27]

Designers build their brand around escapist imagery centered on the ideals of beauty, glamour, and style. Fat, unfortunately, does not fit in with these ideals because it is not beautiful, glamorous, or stylish. Fat is not cool and sexy. Fat is not fashionable. For some designers, any connection with fatness would tarnish their brand image. As a result, they limit their designs to no larger than a size ten or twelve.

There are exceptions of course—if a customer has enough cash to order custom-designed clothes. When Velvet D'Amour entered a designer atelier in France, she noticed the large forms of their regular clientele. Velvet was impressed that there was a curvy Princess "So-and-So," who had her own form there, as well as several other forms of fat women. At a price, one can get haute couture fashions:

> The notion that because Gaultier put me on the runway, therefore he should open, you know, a size twenty-eight plus-size line immediately or he's a total dick, is kind of laughable because, the echelon of people capable to afford haute couture is so limited. I am not saying they shouldn't make them. I would love it if they did, but I also know that if I go in and I have eight billion dollars in my pocket, someone will make something for me.

With regard to the ordinary consumer, more retailers acknowledge the growth potential of the plus-size clothing market and expand their offerings to lure a new customer that, traditionally, has been underserved.[28] Independent designer Jen Wilder understood this potential, being a larger woman herself. "As a plus-size woman," she explained, "I saw a void in the market that under-designed, underappreciated and under-marketed to us."[29] After her straight-size line failed during the recession of 2008, Wilder switched to an exclusively plus-size collection. By June 2012, she established an activewear apparel line called Cult of California in Los Angeles.

These fashion brands realized that they could not afford to leave customers behind; yet, size is not the only issue. Spokeswoman for Lane Bryant, Catherine Lippincott, explained:

> Our customer is very fashion-savvy, and she wants the same looks that her size six friend wants. Other designers and retailers have caught on that these women have plenty of money.[30]

While more women can find clothes in their size, they still search for fashion-forward styles and well-fitting garments.

Despite this growth in size offerings, there is room for improvement as retailers enter into unknown territory. Acknowledging failings in an industry that tends to posit plus size as a "lower end" market, the Plus Size Designers Council formed in 1989 to promote plus-size fashions through promotional and educational activities. The council aimed at overhauling the image and perception of the plus-size market.[31] Plus-size model Liz Dillon served as a spokesperson for the council and worked in the area of promoting plus-size fashions. "As a large-size woman, I saw there were better designer clothes available, but they were under-promoted," she recalled.[32] Aided by her experience as both a model with Ford Models and owner and president of Liz Dillon & Associates, a promotions business based in Ossining, New York, Dillon produced fashion shows and image seminars for retailers to promote the plus-size market.

Plus-size promoters, like Dillon and the council, fight not only size prejudice within the design community but also a market marred by apathy. Retail analyst at Equitable Securities Research, Andrew L. Weinberg, explained that "department stores don't want to be bothered with that kind of customer because it just takes too much work. They'll offer a few muumuus, but that's about it."[33] While many of the major, upscale department stores, such as Bloomingdales, Saks Fifth Avenue, Neiman Marcus, and Nordstrom, have "woman" sections devoted to plus-size clothing, more retailers are transferring their plus-size offerings from in-store to online. Tim Gun, former faculty member of Parsons The New School for Design, chief creative officer at Liz Claiborne, Inc., and on-air mentor on the reality television program *Project Runway*, lamented over the styles that remain in stores:

> Go to Lord & Taylor on Fifth Avenue, I think it's the eighth floor, and it's just a department called "Woman." It's rather devastating. You've never seen such hideous clothes in your entire life. I mean, it's simply

appalling. Thank God there are no windows on that floor, because if I were a size eighteen, I'd throw myself right out the window [after seeing those clothes]. It's insulting what these designers do to these women.[34]

Betty Floura, owner and designer of Coco & Juan clothing line based in Los Angeles, California, added:

> The plus-size customer wants fashion, but some buyers have the mentality that plus-size women only want certain things, like big, bold prints. But that's just not true. She wants everything that is available to her peers in other markets, but she wants it to fit. Stores need to offer more fashion, every season.[35]

With the efforts of the council and independent plus-size designers entering the field, plus-size apparel offerings boomed in the 1990s, and new challenges emerged to appease a hungry demographic that had purchasing power.

Designers shifted from producing tent dresses in solid colors to more fitted dresses in a variety of prints, using contemporary fashion trends as a guide. Designers learned that they could lure in their targeted customer by addressing the issues of style and fit and breaking the rule of covering up the fat body. According to Valerie Steele, chief curator at the museum at the Fashion Institute of Technology:

> For so long, there were so many rules for plus-size women—you couldn't wear sleeveless, or bare backs. Now, there's this attitude that you can still wear really nice clothes, and that is encouraging. The industry is responding to people's desires. It is antipuritan, following no party line.[36]

Besides fit and style, the retail market moved to cater to the youth sector of the market.[37] Chris Hanson, executive vice president of sales at Lane Bryant, noticed, "The young customer coming in has changed the business markedly. She's not waiting to lose weight to look good or wear the latest fashions."[38] Plus-size designers adjusted the design of their garments when aiming for the youth market. For example, Valerie Mander, vice president and divisional merchandise manager for lady's apparel at Houston-based Weiner's Department store, explained that junior styles are cut a bit smaller to fit closer to the body because of a shift in thinking among young women:

> The young plus-size customer is more accepting of her body. She doesn't feel that she needs to buy body coverage. She feels she can wear fashion just as her smaller-size counterpart does.[39]

To reach this younger customer, Lane Bryant launched the Venezia Jeans Clothing Co. in 1998, with the help of the V Girls, a group consisting of five young celebrity role models, including plus-size models Mia Tyler, Sophie Dahl, and Kate Dillon.[40]

The company devised this marketing ploy to reach young consumers. "We want a larger share of the market," remarked Chris Hansen, vice president of marketing at Lane Bryant. "We want the customer who shopped Lane Bryant with her large-size aunt when they were eight years old."[41] In addition to profit motives, Lauren Cohen, president of Designs by Lanie Inc. in Rockaway Beach, New York, aimed to bolster the self-esteem of youth. "We want to make them feel young, contemporary and just as elegant as the skinny little girls around, and with a little pizzazz, too."[42]

A Market of and for Their Own

In order to better serve their targeted customers, fashion retailers needed to know their customers. As a fat woman, Liria Mersini, owner and designer of Cello clothing line based in Santa Monica, California, complained, "I am perceived by manufacturers, buyers and the fashion industry as a whole as having no taste."[43] This forced more women, like Mersini and Wilder, to take action and design their own plus-size clothing lines.

The V Girls from Lane Bryant's Venezia Jeans Clothing Co. promotional campaign.

More self-identified plus-size women enter the design field out of pure frustration, making the plus-size design community a unique market of and for their own. As women who identify as plus-size, they may hold the key to challenging contemporary bodily aesthetics that privilege the thin body. These women are at the forefront of addressing the major criticisms of a fat-phobic fashion community. Their intimate firsthand knowledge of the problems plus-size consumers face provides them with an advantage. These designers address the concerns of their customers, aiming to produce fashions that fit properly and look good.

Former plus-size model Nancy Baum, the owner and president of Cherished-Woman.com, an Internet retailer specialized in trendy plus size clothing, explained her transition into selling clothing:

> I was shocked and dismayed at how limited the choices were for women like myself. It was embarrassing and frustrating to show up to work or at a social function and have on the same outfit as my plus size peers. This has happened to me more times than I care to admit.[44]

Another designer, Jessica Svoboda, launched her line SVOBODA because she desired fashionable clothes. "I was tired of sloppy, ill-fitting clothing and baggy jeans," she commented. "SVOBODA is proof that the demand for fashionable finds extends well beyond a size 'double zero.'"[45] Svoboda understood what her customers wanted because she, herself, was a woman with curves. In designing her fashions, she completely altered the garments to better fit a curvy body and relied on visual tricks, such as using larger buttons and thicker waistbands, to create a slenderizing silhouette.[46] Similarly, when The Limited introduced its plus-size line Eloquii, the designers paid special attention to fit, e.g., more fabric was added to the back of skirts to accommodate ample behinds, the diameters of bracelets were increased, and even purses were enlarged to look more proportional on larger bodies.[47]

Adjusting the fit of a garment for curvy women requires molding the fabric to the body, as Pat Hink, merchandise manager of the plus-size line at Denver-based Rocky Mountain Clothing Co., explained, "Designers can't just add fabric to make a garment plus-size . . . It's about body shape."[48] That is why Yuliya Zeltser, designer and creator of Igigi.com, and Catherine Schuller, former plus-size model and image consultant, collaborated on the development of a size system that categorized the body into different shapes, such as the hourglass and the triangle.[49] This system, adopted by other plus-size retailers such as Lane Bryant, revolutionized the market and reaffirmed that the body comes in many different shapes and sizes.

With the rise of the Internet and blogging, customers have an easier time expressing their complaints and providing feedback to designers and retailers. Fashion blogger for Curvy Fashionist, Marie Denee, admitted, "We will give brands feedback on social media and tell them what works. The plus-size woman is now speaking up for what she wants."[50] Yes, the plus-size woman has spoken. She demands both proper fit and style. As these independent designers gain momentum in the fashion marketplace, the women who proudly wear their clothes have the opportunity to challenge hegemonic beauty standards. As long as these designers continue to produce their collections, women will flaunt their bodies in them.

While the plus-size retail market is growing—both in terms of the increase of plus-size specific fashion lines and other brands that are increasing their size offerings—the ultimate goal is an end to this market segmentation on the basis of size. Plus-size is its own market—retailers specializing their lines for larger bodied women. This approach, then, necessarily treats the plus-size individual as a distinct consumer and potentially provides designers and brands, like the aforementioned cases of Lagerfeld and Abercrombie and Fitch, an excuse to ignore them, i.e., it is the "not my market" argument. When Eden Miller found out that her plus-size line Cabiria would be the first of its kind to show at New York Fashion Week, she reflected on her history-making opportunity:

I'm hoping it becomes a non-issue. I hope that it's a beautiful show. I mean, I'll be happy to get press coverage . . . but I'm really hoping that it's seen just as the other offerings at fashion week.[51]

CHOOSE YOUR SHAPE

| Diamond | Hourglass | Figure Eight | Rectangle | Triangle | Oval | Inverted Triangle |

Bodies come in different shapes and sizes. This is a representation of the size system developed by Yuliya Zeltser and Catherine Schuller.

Miller did not want to be singled out as the plus-size line at Fashion Week. She did not want differential treatment. She wanted to be recognized for her contributions to fashion design, regardless of the size of her designs and consumer, and rejected the idea of a separate plus-size fashion industry versus the fashion industry:

> I definitely want to open the door to other designers who have beautiful lines so they can come in with the same standards they place on the straight sizes. Exclusive, but not prohibitive . . . I think that if we as plus designers keep comparing ourselves only to other plus designers, it's circular and closed. There are so many sources to draw upon in the fashion world; I don't see why it should be separate. We are part of the fashion industry.[52]

These plus-size designers, like Miller, created their lines because they felt pushed out and excluded from fashion. These women strove for legitimacy as designers and hope that more clothing lines will begin to cater to plus-size customers.

Fat-Bottomed Girls

For plus-size models, commercial modeling, where the model appears on websites and print media advertisements, can be lucrative in terms of both exposure and compensation. If hired by an established retail company like Lane Bryant or Avenue, a plus-size model can make anywhere from a few hundred to a few thousand dollars per job, as negotiated by her agent. For example, Lane Bryant primarily hires models from either Ford Models or Wilhelmina Models and flies them to corporate headquarters in Ohio for weeklong product shoots. Since it relies on models provided by an agency, Lane Bryant hires models who are no larger than a size fourteen or sixteen, since the agencies themselves do not have larger models. Similarly, Avenue, which retails fashion-forward women's clothing in sizes fourteen to thirty-two both in stores and online through its website (www.avenue.com), also hires its models from the same professional modeling agencies as Lane Bryant; yet, the models in Avenue Body's lingerie advertisements are visibly smaller than those used in Lane Bryant's advertisements.

On the other hand, fledgling plus-size retailers often rely on a local consumer base to work as hired models, and usually these models are reimbursed for their time in either cash or merchandise. This is the case with Plus Size Plum Lingerie, a web-based retail site of "sexy plus size lingerie for big, beautiful, women who radiate humor, style and intelligence." Founded by former plus-size model, Deborah Friedman, Plus Size Plum Lingerie offers a collection of intimate apparel that will "enhance the beautiful plum in all of us." Due to its location in Durham, North Carolina, Plus Size Plum Lingerie has limited access to plus-size models. Consequently, the owner, Deborah Friedman, and her husband scout for women to model on their website at local restaurants and shopping centers.

Similar to boutiques that scout from among their customers to model in in-store fashion shows, some retailers invite customers to submit their photos for consideration through an online submission process. Hips and Curves, for example, scouts for models for upcoming photo shoots through its website. An exclusive web-based business, Hips and Curves caters to curvy women, offering its exclusively plus-size clientele the latest in lingerie since operations began in 2000. Owner Rebecca Jennings encourages her consumers to submit their pictures (one close-up and one full body shot) via email or mail. Prospective models must be women who wear at least a size twelve, "*love* wearing sexy lingerie" [emphasis theirs], and live in Southern California, where its administrative offices and call center are located. Hips and Curves prefers to use local models for ease of availability in the case of last-minute photo shoots.

Whether using professional plus-size models or women off of the street, all plus-size lingerie retailers seek to use models whom their customers can both identify with and aspire to, as well as capture the look of the clothes. Above all, the models embody brand aesthetics. When Jennings, from Hips and Curves, requires her models "*love* wearing sexy lingerie," she is not simply scouting on the sole basis of physical appearance. She looks for women who fit her brand image in terms of their energy, i.e., affective labor. Jennings wants models who would be interested in her clothes even outside of the context of the job. Similarly, during a casting for an independent, web-based plus-size collection, the designer team asked me if I had examined their offerings on their website before the meeting and, if I had, which article of clothing was my favorite. They were asking these questions to gauge my enthusiasm for a product I would be selling if hired for the job. This was their way of determining if I would be able to embody their brand aesthetics to become their brand's ambassador. Selecting a model for an advertising campaign or catalog is not simply a matter of who looks the best. It is a highly subjective process that involves discerning the worker's potential to embody an organization's values—its image—through her look, mannerisms, voice, and style.

Additionally, the types of bodies used in these images are of growing concern to the consumer. More of the newer, web-based retailers have begun using "larger" plus-size models. For instance, the models on the

Plus Size Plum website come in a wider range of sizes than nationally franchised clothing retailers. As owner Deborah Friedman explained in a personal correspondence:

> I prefer to use size sixteen models so my customers can identify with them. I've had complaints in the past that our models didn't look plus-size enough. I actually used a size twenty-two for some pictures.

Competing with national retailers who do not use models larger than a size sixteen, these newer brands do not want to risk alienating consumers. Similarly, Luscious Plus Lingerie stresses its use of a variety of plus-size bodies to potential customers on its website, "As you explore the site you will be able to relate to the ladies in media photos, product photos, which further illustrates our dedication to luscious women :-)"[53] The website prominently features "larger" plus-size models on its homepage.

Hiring "smaller" plus-size models may alienate consumers, who may perceive it as a mismatch between a brand's aesthetics and the models' bodies. As sociologist Kjerstin Gruys discovered during her ethnographic research at a plus-size clothing store, customers are sensitive to the size of bodies, even the size of store employees. At a store she initially described as "an oasis of body acceptance," most of the employees were plus size; however, some, like Gruys who wore a size ten, were standard size.[54] While working at the store as an employee, Gruys overheard a customer request to speak with a manager:

> The woman said, "Well, that's just it . . . you might not understand. I haven't been in here for a while, so maybe something changed, but isn't this supposed to be a store for big ladies? All of the girls working here are small. Didn't they used to be bigger?" . . . The woman looked upset, and asked "but isn't this a store for bigger girls?" . . . The customer left the store without looking at anything, saying, "I'll come back another day, but I hope it's back to normal by then."[55]

Web-based retailers, such as Luscious Plus Lingerie seen here, tend to use larger plus-size models than nationally franchised brands.

As Gruys notes, this customer expected to see plus-size workers at a plus-size store. When her expectations were not met, she left the store without making a purchase. Similarly, Friedman, from Plus Size Plum, feared for her business after a similar reaction from customers, so she rectified her mistake. By using larger models on its websites, online-only brands like Plus Size Plum and Luscious Plus Lingerie seek to appeal to a more diverse range of women by using models of various sizes (while brands with physical retail space use larger sales associates as well). These models are curvier and rounder than those who typically appear in print for national retailers. The owners of these online boutiques aim to show their products on "real" bodies.

In the past two decades, plus-size retail expanded, offering more brands, larger sizes, and utilizing plus-size models with increased girth.

With the growth of e-commerce, plus-size designers reached a larger pool of consumers via the Internet with greater ease. Independent labels and boutique owners rely on online sales to increase profit margins and expand their business nationwide. While designers hire thin models to promote their fashion and appeal to a targeted young and thin demographic, online fashion catalogs tend to feature models of size sixteen through size twenty-four to appeal to a larger clientele. The arguably "larger" plus-size model, shunned by certain sectors of the fashion industry, gains visibility in a burgeoning virtual marketplace.

Flesh Exposed

The aims of plus-size lingerie retailers are not different from other general lingerie retailers, such as Victoria's Secret, except that they cater to a specific niche market based on size. Marketing lingerie involves highlighting an idealized femininity, one that is characteristically thin. While sexuality is implicit for thin models, plus-size models present a more explicit sexuality in order to counter the stigma of asexuality. To do so, marketing efforts place greater emphasis on an overt sexuality.

Intimate apparel accentuates rounded breasts and hips and intensifies the wearer's femininity. Flesh is exposed; the normally hidden is placed on full, prominent display. The wearer cannot hide behind her shapewear. So, in order to attract fat women, retailers present a retooled image of a fat body. The plus-size women presented by these lingerie retailers idealize the stigma of fat by exposing that which the cultural discourse tries to make invisible. Plus-size lingerie retailers expose the woman's body to reveal her flesh and sensual curves, presenting a new image of a fat woman embracing her body. These images expose the flesh and show plus-size models proudly flaunting their fat amid a cultural discourse that seeks to cover it in shame. This new image entices fat women to shed the layers of shame and timidity that formed under the pressure of a stigma.

This body-accepting branding serves as a beauty counter-discourse. For example, marketing campaigns infuse a seductive sensuality and overt sexuality into their presentations. Consumers are presented with a sensual image of the fat woman, as evidenced in Avenue Body's "Sexy Nights" campaign, "Own the night in our collection of seductive lingerie that will help you to flirt with desire and romance the mysterious."[56] These models smile with their eyes while curling their lips as if they have a secret to share with the consumer. They lean against a backdrop, emphasizing their curves. Similarly, Hips and Curves "celebrates the beauty and sensuality of fuller figures" and offers something on its website "for every seductress."[57] In a lacy bra and panty set, a model reclines on a windowsill, running her fingers through her hair. With pursed lips, she soaks in the sun's rays. We, the consumer, furtively look into this private moment of seduction.

The serious sensuality of these models contrasts with the mirth and levity of those used in Cacique advertisements. Counter to the idea that larger women should wear black and other dark colors to camouflage their size and shape, plus-size lingerie comes in a variety of colors. Instead of hiding, women are encouraged to call attention to their more ample features with bright colors. In one Cacique advertising campaign, women are urged to "get sexy and playful" and to "color their curves," as one model wears a blue tank top with "sassy" written across the chest and another model poses flirtatiously with her back to the camera to reveal "aloha" written on the backside of her panty. The message is that fat women can be playful and sensual like any other woman of any size without being too risqué. These models laugh, smile, and flirtatiously beckon the consumer with a pout of the lip. They do not cover up their bodies. They flaunt them.

According to advertising campaigns such as these, fat women can be playful and flirtatious, be sensual and seductive, and engage in sexual role-play. Plus-size lingerie retailers offer an array of corsets, bustiers, costumes, and other fantasy items. For the daring woman, corsets are not a thing of the past, according to Hips and Curves:

> Today's femme fatales have ditched the whalebones of the 1400s in favor of
> softly cinching plus size corsets and plus size bustiers that celebrate their

An advertisement for Hips and Curves that utilizes seductive sensuality to sell lingerie to plus-size women.

This Cacique advertisement, "Color Your Curves," stresses the playful and flirtatious side of plus-size women.

curves while offering support and style. Channel your Marilyn Monroe and show off your hourglass figure in an über sexy plus size bustier, plus size corset or merry widow.[58]

With a corset or costume, a woman can unleash her inner sexpot and enter the realm of fantasy.

Offering a selection of lingerie sets, a variety of bras and panties, baby-dolls, nightgowns, bustiers, chemises, and body stockings, plus-size lingerie retailers seek to supply women with intimate garments that fit and flatter the larger body. Curvy Couture, for example, focuses on the fit of its lingerie:

> Because we understand curvy women, we know that the fit of your curvy underwear matters. For that reason we provide not only a wide range of sizes to choose from, but create every curvy bra and panty with support, comfort and fit in mind. From microfiber technology in your under-wire bra, to lightly lined tummy control panties, you can be sure that we always aim to make you comfortable and help you get the right fit for your curves.[59]

The collection aims to "enhance and support a curvy woman's natural curves" because "you and your curves are sexy, so flatter them!" Sculptresse by Panache also gears its products to a plus-size customer who is concerned with form and function. It offers special design features such as a smooth-shaped wing, cushioned hook and eye closure, and fully adjustable straps that sit closer together on the shoulder.

Ultimately, these retailers provide fat women with options that traditional retailers have not. The brand summary statement by Luscious Plus Lingerie sums up these aims:

> You are Bodacious, Bold & Beautiful. Whether you want to pamper your-self, treading outside of your comfort zone, adding a little spice into your life or exploring new intimacy trends, we have something just for you and

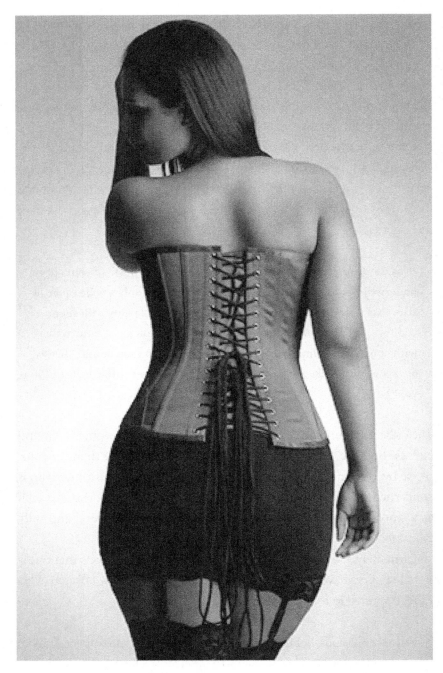

The corset re-imagined for the plus-size woman, by Hips and Curves.

in your size . . . Luscious Plus Lingerie LLC is setting new standards of
sexiness for our curvy ladies, allowing you to feel just as sexy and sensual
as anyone else, we are vastly moving away from the limitations of floppy
flower prints, to steamy leather, popular animal prints, glittered items,
two-piece sets and an inventory of full figured sexy, silky, laced up corsets
and much, much more.[60]

By presenting consumers with the image of a sexually charged curvy
woman, these retailers attempt to recapture the lost femininity of a fat
woman and transform her into an empowered woman, empowered
enough to make a purchase. As a woman seeks bras and lingerie that
hug her curves and support her breasts, plus-size lingerie companies offer
her a variety of options, from plain and sturdy to sexy and lacy. A woman
of any size can potentially transform herself into an object of desire and
enter her own fantasy.

The presence of these provocative images and rise of plus-size models expand the fashion landscape and challenge cultural conceptions of
beauty. As the plus-size model gains status in the modeling industry, she
also becomes more visible to consumers. Posing within magazines and on
the web, a plus-size model presents an alternative image of a fat woman
that is designed to soften the stigma of fat. Instead of covering up their fat,
these plus-size models strip down and arch their backs to emphasize their
curves. An advertisement for Sculptresse by Panache exemplifies this type
of imagery. The model, dressed in a bright pink bra and panty set, assumes
a pose reminiscent of a 1950s pinup girl, complete with a parasol.

The highly stylized image in the ad calls for a rejection of bodily shame
and respect for feminine beauty. Kneeling before the viewer, she tilts her
head to expose the sensual curves of her neck. While this body positioning speaks of vulnerability, she still commands attention. She smiles with
a come-hither stare. Flesh is exposed, and the viewer is challenged to see
all of her plus-size body as sexual, desirable, and beautiful.

While this performance of fat appears to support a form of sexual liberation for plus-size women, it is really an act of reproducing

An advertisement for Sculptresse by Panache that exemplifies the use of 1950s pinup girl imagery.

heteronormative bodily ideals and what Samantha Murray calls "an obsession with the visible."[61] Her very pose is an imitation of sexual displays of women throughout the twentieth century and today. The Sculptresse brand, itself, is a "fuller-figured" version of Panache lingerie; Cacique is a facsimile of its "little" sister Victoria's Secret. The look of her curvy (yet smoothed and toned) body, aided with properly fitting and stylish lingerie, is of the utmost importance as fashion continues to privilege aesthetic ideals. Fashion commodifies and reduces this model to a sexual object subject to the male gaze. The difference, however, is that the branding message teaches her that she is as desirable as a "thin" model. In the end, there is no counter aesthetic presented in these images—just differently sized bodies.

Bodies Behind an Image

In the marketing of intimate apparel, the commodified fat body becomes embodied and visualized in order to attract (1) an underserved niche market that is (2) on a quest for better fit and style options in order to (3) bring sexy back to the full-figured. The sexualization of the fat body is an attempt to reclaim femininity and beauty amid a fat-phobic society. Plus-size retailers create a new image to attract a fashion-starved demographic. In exposing the taboo of the fat body, these images tell us that plus-size models, even if they are fat, are beautiful and sexy. These plus-size models convey this message of body acceptance through affective labor. Retailers hope that the intended consumer connects with the image and makes a purchase, thus legitimizing this carefully constructed visual plan to overhaul the dominant cultural discourse on fat.

These marketing campaigns contain an inspirational component. On set, the photography team invites the models to imagine themselves as seductive characters and pose for the camera in slinky lingerie. These characters can be kinky, provocative, but, ultimately, imaginary. The images of these plus-size models are airbrushed, retouched, and altered. Extra rolls of skin are smoothed and removed. In the end, the images displayed on these lingerie websites present a retooled fat body that is, at last, acceptable, but imitations of heteronormative constructions of beauty.

In the final chapter, I conclude with a discussion of what is absent from these fantastical images of exposed flesh and exaggerated curves—the backstage labor process involved in creating these images and a concern for health. Amid this retooled deviant body that is purposefully sexualized, there is no mention of the aesthetic labor these models engage in to achieve that image, nor is there mention of the increased risk for heart disease and diabetes among fat women. Fashion professionals present a marketable image of a "plus-size" beauty in a desirable, slick, and superficially happy package, hiding her flaws, physical labor, and health concerns from consumers.

7

Stepping Out of the Plus-Size Looking Glass

I walked up the steps of "Fashion Hall" in midtown Manhattan. As workers literally rolled out the red carpet in preparation for the night's main event, I scampered up the steps to seek shelter from the gentle drizzle. Once inside, I found myself in a gilded hall amidst a process of transformation, echoing one that I, too, was to undergo that afternoon. In four hours, I would walk down a fashion runway.

As production staff dashed around, setting up chairs along the constructed runway, I headed to the rear of the hall toward the makeshift backstage area. Behind the partitions, three plus-size models awaited instructions as Michelle, the style director for the fashion show, scurried in and out of the ladies room. She was busy fitting a model for a morning show appearance the next day. As she multitasked, we—the models for the show that evening—waited. Throughout the afternoon, eight more models arrived to participate in the evening's festivities.

Half an hour later, an assistant instructed us to head over to hair and makeup. As the hair stylists and makeup crew set up, the thought of my forthcoming debut on a New York City runway overwhelmed me. *Feeling like a fish out of water, could I really pull this off? Would my inexperience be evident on the catwalk? While I had previously "worked the runway" at a Seventeen/Macy's event, that was almost a decade ago. Could I really do this now?*

I plopped into the first chair for hair. The hair stylist decided on a "loose 'do with a flip." She slathered a volumizing cream on the top of my head and rolled the top layers of hair in Velcro rollers. While the rollers set, she shooed me over to makeup. Once in the makeup chair, the makeup artist applied a base layer of foundation on my face with a sponge and fluffed powder atop my nose and across my forehead.

As the makeup artist attended to my eyes, a production assistant gave us a ten-minute warning for our runway rehearsal and reminded us to wear our heels to practice our strut. While the other models rushed to their garment bags to change into their heels, I remained in my chair. Perhaps indicative of modeling inexperience or a by-product of living day-to-day in style-centric New York, I had been wearing a pair of "sexy, thin-heeled" ankle boots, a staple in my winter wardrobe, the entire time.

As we headed to the staging area, an unabashed, flamboyant runway specialist named Charleston greeted us. "Walk in your natural groove and have fun," he reassured us. "We want big smiles," he commanded. Charleston demonstrated our route down the runway, indicating the points where we were to pose and turn. Then, it was our turn to walk down the catwalk.

As we each took our turn, he became our personal cheerleader, lauded us on our sass, and encouraged us to have fun. It was my turn. With my hair still in curlers, I held my head up high and struck my first pose. As the model before me turned to head off the stage, I stepped forward and strutted down the runway, as Charleston cried out, "Fierce . . . oh, you know you're fierce!"

Back in the makeup chair, the makeup artist finished lining my eyes for a smoky eye look and brushed a raspberry tinted gloss onto my lips. "You have a great walk, my love. You're a natural," she assured me as she applied the finishing touches. Next, I headed back to the hair station, where the hair stylist removed the Velcro rollers and brushed, fluffed, and sprayed my hair into place.

Earlier, Michelle had left to retrieve our wardrobe for the show. Someone had prearranged a bike messenger to deliver a couple thousand dollars worth of dresses to the event, but, since it was raining, Michelle took a car to pick them up and avert a fashion disaster. Less than an hour and a half until we were scheduled to hit the runway, she had not returned with our little black dresses. We waited and finished our primping in hair and makeup.

With less than an hour until show time, Michelle finally arrived with the dresses, and we scurried to finish our transformations. While huddled behind the runway, Michelle's assistant doled out the dresses to us. She handed me the smallest dress in her arsenal, one that was at least two sizes too big. I tried it on and, luckily, due to the color and the type of material, the designer halter dress gracefully draped my frame. Afterward, we moved to the accessory station. The stylist handed me a scarlet, beaded necklace with a golden pendant and logged it in her ledger.

At six o'clock, the stage manager instructed us to line up, where I was assigned the second spot in the lineup. Ten minutes later, the production team hushed the atmosphere music, and an announcer called the audience's attention to the stage. Donning a black lace dress, Michelle stepped out from behind the scrim onto the runway. She welcomed the enthusiastic crowd and introduced the collection. The stage manager directed the first model to start and told me to hit my first mark, i.e., step out onto the runway and pose.

As I emerged from behind the scrim, a stream of blinding flashes illuminated my silhouette as I struck my first pose. *Smile. Have fun. Oh, and don't trip!* I heard the music pumping, and internalized the beat to use as a guide for my walk.

I took my first step down the runway.

Michelle introduced me to the crowd and detailed my outfit. As I stopped to pose again at the top of the runway, photographers fiercely focused their cameras on me to capture the look in that moment. The thrill of all the attention intoxicated me. With Michelle's voice floating over the music, I soaked in my moment. I felt fierce.

Objects in the Spectacle of Fashion

My short glimpse into the realm of modeling revealed this illusion. With each click of a camera or strut down a runway, the spectacle seduced me.

As a model pampered and dressed in the latest fashions, I attest to the ease with which a model may get lost in the moment and feel liberated from a stigma. Under the spell of a "cultural goal of becoming photographable," I no longer felt like an ordinary woman.[1] As a model, I believed that I was special, a standout among the crowd, and no longer burdened by my failure to live up to the engendered bodily ideal of thinness. As models of resistance against a negative cultural discourse surrounding the fat body, these women expose their bodies of curves without shame. For those brief moments, they emerge victorious, reclaim their femininity, and feel empowered.

Instead, behind the image, we have neglected plus-size models. Fashion marginalizes these plus-size models within a system of work embedded in a complex web of power relations and practices. The beauty thought collective—comprised of modeling agents, fashion designers, photographers, and advertising executives—defines what is beautiful (and marketable). The only one who does not have a voice is the model, herself.

Without concern for their health or self-image beyond capturing the look of confidence in a photo or on the runway, critical-eyed modeling agents push their models to bodily management extremes. The agent invests in the model's body, and it is her body capital that books jobs and earns money for both her and her agency. From tracking each body measurement to dictating to them how to present themselves to clients, agents are in control of their models' careers. Plus-size models become products that agents fix up and dress up to present to clients as desirable packages. Agents sell these manufactured packages to clients, who in turn resell them to consumers. The models, themselves, lose their creative voice, selling a client's vision that is not their own.

A plus-size model labors over her body landscape, haunted by a continual sense of imperfection. Whether her body is a source of embarrassment and shame or prideful accomplishment, overwhelmingly, it is something she must control and master. The aesthetics of the body is her focus. Like Bakhtin's grotesque body, she continually acts within the private sphere upon an emergent body that is in a persistent state of generation and restoration.[2] She works to increase the utility of her body. She works to improve the internal functions, as well as alter the external façade. She becomes an object within the spectacle of fashion.

Illusion of Embodiment

Amid our consumer culture, cultural theorist Jean Baudrillard argues that the mode of relation to the body is a narcissistic one:

> It is a *managed* narcissism, operating on the body as in colonized virgin "territory," "affectionately" [*tendrement*] exploring the body like a deposit to be mined in order to extract from it the visible signs of happiness, health, beauty, and the animality which triumphs in the marketplace of fashion . . . One manages one's body; one handles it as one might handle an inheritance; one manipulates it as one of the many *signifiers of social status*.[3]

The body becomes significant as both capital and consumer object, with standardized ideas of beauty as the goal.

According to this logic, we, the public audience, assume that, because of their size, plus-size models suffer from a "sin by omission," i.e., failure to keep up with necessary engendered bodily devotional practices.[4] However, unbeknownst to the public, they do indeed discipline themselves and engage in regimented practices as part of an aesthetic labor process.

While these plus-size models engage in at times severe bodily management practices, the public outside of the fashion industry has no knowledge of it. This public is not privy to the model's intimate disciplines. That is part of the fantasy portrayed by the fashion industry—to show a final image without revealing all the work that goes into its production. The public is only allowed to see a commercial persona—a constructed image of the plus-size woman.[5] The aesthetic labor process creates this commercial persona—one ripe with sexuality. Exposing the flesh, these images show a plus-size model embracing her fat, flaunting her stigma.

While plus-size models actively manage their fat bodies, they still face stigmatization because they are not meant to reveal exactly that which may serve to counter the presumption of laziness and lack of discipline associated with fat in the cultural discourse. Ultimately, there is little hope of changing the cultural discourse toward fat and plus-size models, as long as the bodily practices of plus-size models remain hidden from public view.

This study captured the discrepancy between the public staged performance of fat and the hidden backstage aesthetic labor process in plus-size modeling. In this intense aesthetic labor process, these models utilize their body as capital, embark on a variety of body projects, and, ultimately, reproduce heteronormative imperatives involving female bodies. In cultivating themselves as models, these women engage in engendered body projects designed to control their fat and, ultimately, reinforce their sense of disembodiment.

The self-surveillance and corporal discipline required of this aesthetic labor process is antithetical to the task of reclaiming one's embodiment because the body is still an object that the model must control and master. As "docile" bodies, plus-size models engage in a constant battle to control and discipline their flesh. They develop a repertoire of specialized professional techniques to increase their "model physical capital." Technologies of control, such as a tape measure, legitimize and normalize this constant surveillance of each curve. As part of the physical strategies employed by plus-size models to remain marketable to clients, models track each measurement and manipulate their bodies by either invasive or non-invasive techniques, ranging from strict dieting and exercise to wearing padding in the appropriate places. As women, plus-size models continue to manage and manipulate their bodies in hopes of appealing to fashion's elite.

Plus-size models emulate a work ethic dominated by the normative values of self-discipline, inner strength, and diligence. While plus-size models invest in their bodies, they alienate the self and transform their bodies into manipulated and consumed objects. There is no subversion because preexisting aesthetic ideals direct this process of self-cultivation. Plus-size models assume the same come-hither poses and piercing looks as straight-size models. They try to claim their space in fashion without presenting a counter-aesthetic. The singular difference is the size of the bodies. Plus-size models and agents aim to expand the notion of beauty to include *bodies* of different sizes, but that does not eliminate the problem of disembodiment because these women, whether straight-or plus-size, are simply bodies. Fashion still judges these women on the basis of their looks. Modeling reduces them to curves, numbers on a tape measure. They are not women but breasts and hips. The models' reclamation of embodiment is an illusion. After all their aesthetic labor, plus-size models are still disembodied, fat bodies.

Full-Figure Disclosure

This study presents us with a unique example of how labor processes can extend beyond the confines of work, affect the social identity of workers, and aid in the production of fantasy. Other body-centric professionals—dancers, athletes, exotic dancers, and fitness instructors—adopt techniques of bodily control that affect not only their performance of work but their lived experience. Fitness instructors, too, must inhabit a fit body, i.e., corporally demonstrating the effectiveness of an exercise regimen, or they may lose their clientele. Professional singers engage in ritualized vocal techniques to maintain their instrument even when not in performance mode, e.g., strict vocal rests, wearing scarves around their necks to keep their vocal cords warm, and consuming beverages and foods designed to soothe their voices. Method actors embrace their characters on and off the film set by physically altering their bodies for a role and refusing to break out of character in between takes.

Yet, contrary to a dancer or boxer who trains his or her body toward an established aesthetic—an athletic, lean, and strong body—plus-size models work within the confines of a cultural field of tastemakers to create aesthetics. From affective, emotional, to physical labor, the work process of plus-size models not only increases the utility of a body but also functions to assist the production of an image. As such, they have a role in (but not control of) molding cultural constructions of fatness. The structure of modeling, like many body-centric fields, is essentially a network of differential relations between social actors that involves both a highly developed canon of body techniques and those social actors who can synthesize these techniques.[6] Fashion models develop their bodies according to the requirements of the field, as dictated by their agents. Models embody an aesthetic.

Today's plus-size models represent a diversity of shapes and sizes—from hourglass to triangle and size ten to size twenty-four. They display their curvy bodies with pride. They stand in direct opposition to the stigmatizing image of the fat woman depicted in cultural discourse. Erving Goffman reminds us that the stigmatized individual is "not a type or a category, but a human being."[7] When dealing with "normals," Goffman reveals that it may become necessary to remind them of the stigmatized humanity and pursue a course of action that reduces the tension. In this sense, plus-size models are not just fat bodies with spoiled identities. They are women who want to be seen for more than their weight. They want to be seen as beautiful. They want to grab your attention because they are special for reasons both related to and beyond their physical stature. But, plus-size models are more than "happy fat girls," as freelance model Yvonne wryly generalized the conception of plus-size models portrayed by the industry. Plus-size models smolder in provocative lingerie that displays all of their flesh. These models make a statement.

By appearing in advertisements that sexualize and emphasize their curves, plus-size models work for cultural producers whose objective is to boost retail clothing sales. Consequently, these models represent a movement to reevaluate the negative discourse on fat. These depictions of curvy bodies reflect a more positive image of larger bodies. These carefully crafted images reveal a fun, flirty, and fashionable woman but hide the active work done *by* and *on* her.

Remember, however, a plus-size model is not an average woman. A fashion expert chose her for her symmetrical facial features and proportional frame. Upon entering the field, she is the agent's blank canvas. Then, a slew of aesthetic professionals—her agent, photographers, stylists, makeup artists, and hair professionals—work *on* her. Only then does her body idealize a fat body. It takes a team and strict adherence to the demands of aesthetic labor to create a desirable image.

The resulting image of this aesthetic process is an illusion. First, photographers and image editors manipulate the image either by airbrushing or photoshopping, a practice exposed in Dove's Evolution commercial. The image captures the fat body, so to speak, in the best light. A three hundred-pound woman, like Velvet D'Amour, with professionally styled hair and makeup, the proper lighting, camera angles, and positioning of the body, can be subjectively considered, in her own words, "hot" and appeal to a wide audience. Second, the bodies, themselves, are not sustainable in the long run without medical complications. Given the extremes to which she goes to maintain her body size and shape, a fashion model jeopardizes her health and well-being. The fashion industry swings from one extreme in weight to another, and models must adjust their bodies accordingly in order to remain marketable.[8]

Too Fat and Too Skinny

For many plus-size models, Velvet D'Amour, at nearly three hundred pounds, is an icon. They applauded her for her confident strut down the runway, and many models used her photography as inspiration for their own work in front of the camera. Fashion critics even crowned her as "today's super-sized hero" for ordinary women.[9]

Velvet's emergence on the runway coincided with the skinny model debate that erupted within the fashion industry following the deaths of two South American anorectic models, Uruguayan Luisel Ramos and Brazilian Ana Carolina Reston.[10] Several of the major fashion capitals considered instituting preventative measures after these sudden deaths.

For example, Spain took action by first banning ultra-thin models from fashion week and then banning skinny sizes on mannequins.[11] In New York, Bronx Assemblyman Jose Rivera proposed the creation of a state advisory board that would establish weight guidelines for the fashion and entertainment industries.[12] In 2012, the Council of Fashion Designers of America urged designers to ensure that their runway models were not younger than age sixteen.[13] Unfortunately, most of these proposed initiatives from around the fashion globe did little to decrease the prevalence of eating disorders among fashion models. Britain tried to ban size zero models from London Fashion Week, but that was quickly abandoned after other fashion capitals failed to follow suit.[14] Anorectic looking models still parade down the runways to the cheers of celebrities and the fashion elite.

In response to this skinny ban bandwagon and the mixed reception she received after modeling for Jean Paul Gaultier, Velvet explained:

> I've had people ask me "Do you think you are promoting obesity by you being on the runway?" I think it's laughable. If what's on the runway had anything to do with obesity then we would all be emaciated.[15]

While Velvet disagreed with a model's impact on the general public's eating behavior, ultra-skinny models who walk the runway and appear in magazines do have an influence. Studies demonstrate that young girls develop eating disorders while attempting to emulate the thin physiques of high-fashion models.[16] As plus-size models become more prominent in fashion, more questions arise about the dangers of fat.

Plus-size models, like Velvet, are frustrated by the lack of diversity in fashion and the incongruity of treatment between plus- and straight-size models. She experienced this differential treatment after submitting her calendar to several women's magazines. All but one rejected her request for publicity. Velvet revealed:

> I am too obese to be okay. It doesn't really matter what I have done, you know, in their mind, like, they would be promoting unhealth by touching

me . . . That sort of accepted mythology of looking upon a thin model and publicizing that person from here to kingdom come, based on what they perceive as is healthy versus, you know, I go swimming 120 laps and don't have high blood pressure. I never smoke. I never drink. I don't do drugs. I just think it is so hypocritical to me that they can put models in magazines, who, on occasion, walk off the runway and keel over. So, how is that healthy?

Yes, how are any of the bodies of fashion considered healthy? When, if at all, does the issue of health come into play? The answer is simple—never. The fantastical images that emphasize the sensuality of ample curves omit the health risks associated with maintaining a static body size at all costs. The aesthetic labor process, itself, demands that a model ignore the dangers associated with forcing her body to fit a desired mold. These are manufactured bodies shaped to fit an aesthetic value without concern for how they were created.[17]

Fashion perceives these models as voiceless bodies with dyeable hair and fixable features. If their measurements are not in perfect proportion, they stick padding onto their hips or "chicken cutlets" onto their breasts and squeeze them into a pair of Spanx. Photoshop eliminates the remaining imperfections, such as acne, cellulite, and extra rolls of flesh. Agents take their plus-size models to dinner, encouraging them to eat and gain weight. If a fit model loses weight, she is told to do whatever it takes to gain the weight back before the next fitting, even if that means binging on fat-laden foods that can wreak havoc on an individual's body. If these efforts fail, the client and/or agent will easily replace them. The organizational structure within the field of fashion conceals the destructive potential of these severe bodily management practices. "Whatever it takes" is the unofficial mantra, all behind the camera and hidden from the consumer's view.

I Came, I Saw, I Was Conquered

My brief time as a model paralleled the journey of many others, a path marked by doubt, discomfort, thrill, and a whole lot of rejection. I began without a clear sense of my marketability or possession of basic modeling skills. I knew little about fashion. Yet, I dreamed of my image emblazoned on a billboard in Times Square. These starry-eyed thoughts of fame danced around my imagination, prompting me to make one more call or send another email in hopes someone would "discover" me.

While none of these fantasies came to fruition, I experienced the world of fashion from the inside. I stepped in front of the camera and onto the runway. I peeked behind the curtain and found women who yearned for a fashion authority to recognize their intelligence, confidence, and beauty. They wanted to change the way people thought about beauty, diversifying its definition to include curvy bodies. They championed for size acceptance. Ultimately, they remained voiceless dolls, dependent on agencies to direct their careers and clients to mold their image. Instead of challenge a social system that perpetuated preoccupation with the body, these plus-size models reified it. In order to succeed, they altered their bodies according to others' specifications. If we want to seek out actors who challenge hegemonic beauty standards, we must look elsewhere. Instead of the objects in the billboards, we must look to the designers of those billboards.

I journeyed into a fantastical world governed by strict aesthetic rules. According to its logic, I was no longer considered an average body type but, rather, "plus size." One agent urged me to "stay the same [weight]," while another presented me with an option to either gain or lose weight. Given these conflicting messages, I wondered whether I could be myself—accept my body—in this industry. Was this experience empowering me or, alternatively, suppressing me? When women like me seek personal validation by entering a field dominated by aesthetics, what does it say about our culture and its fixation on physical appearance? Why did I need someone to say, "Yes, you are pretty enough to model"?

Despite my academic credentials, the engendered cultural pressures to embody beauty continued to weigh down my self-esteem. I envisioned that this opportunity would finally silence my internal critic. To an extent, it did. I rocked the fashion runway and learned how to accentuate my assets. These experiences and gained aesthetic knowledge empowered me—to a point.

After many years of neglecting my body to focus on mental pursuits within an academic setting, I felt uncomfortable and overwhelmed by the continual focus on the physical body in a fashion setting. From the moment I entered the fashion district, strangers wrapped tape measures around my body, styled my look, and paraded me before an audience. No one asked for my thoughts and opinions. I had simply gone from one extreme to another—from books to looks.

As a woman, I felt enough everyday cultural pressure to "do looks." I no longer wanted to compulsively measure my bust, hips, and waist and enslave myself to a number on the bathroom scale. I tired of the unpredictability and need to be in a constant state of readiness—always groomed and fashionably dressed—to drop everything and run to a casting at my agent's beck and call. I was simply not interested in doing beauty *all* the time.

Soon after my jaunt down the runway and a series of failed castings, my size became an issue. I was too small. In order to continue modeling, I needed to gain weight so that my body would fit into a plus-size sample size. Given fashion's unpredictability, I may have had to then lose weight in the future to match new aesthetic demands. I did not want to play these kinds of body games. How could I be authentically me while continually manipulating my physical body according to clients' specifications? Changing my body to meet the requirements of another is antithetical to the pursuit of embodiment.

In the end, I (and my body) retreated in defeat, refusing to match the aesthetic ideal required for plus-size modeling. The larger cultural discourse that fosters bodily insecurity and hegemonic body standards won. I could not willingly act to make my body larger. I rationalized that my role was not to embody the changing face of beauty but to understand its construction; however, truthfully, the stigma of fat was too great.

As I now sit, comfortable within the halls of academia, I recall the sight of plus-size models gathered together in the hallways of a Manhattan studio, waiting for their chance to wow the casting directors. These women laughed together, shared work-related horror stories, and showed off their skills in impromptu posing contests. While I sat with them, feeling nervous and out of place due to my lack of experience and aesthetic knowledge, I marveled at their confidence and sheer joy at a casting. I wanted to experience that level of festivity, as well. Their glee, however, understated a painful journey of self-discovery. As Chris, a size fourteen/sixteen model, revealed:

> I struggled with self-esteem for many years due to my weight. I was bigger than everyone. I didn't look like everyone else . . . Even when I first started [modeling], it was difficult—all that rejection. I had to learn to not take it personally. When I started to book jobs, it was a huge boost. I began to get comfortable with my size. Now, I am fine the way I am. I don't want to be a size two . . . As a [plus-size] model, I feel pressure to be a role model, but I accept that. I didn't have someone to look up to growing up that looked like me. I want to represent a positive message and give girls someone to look up to. I accept that mission. We [as plus-size models] need to.

While these plus-size models are marginalized by an industry that treats them as novelties, they focus not only on fighting this resistance to further their careers but also on the impact their presence in fashion has on other women. Models like Chris share the burden of representing self-identified plus-size women. Many did not begin their modeling careers with this intention but often end up embracing the mantle of spokesmodel for body acceptance.

Although I am not on the front lines of the battle to redefine beauty to include more types of bodies, I applaud those who have the courage to withstand fat stigma and bare their flesh for all to see. These curvy women are working diligently to bring sexy back to the full-figured. The plus-size models may not be in control of the image, itself, but it is their bodies that are on display. They are the ones who risk exposure to public ridicule. On the runway, they are alone and vulnerable. Their confidence amidst popular opinion on fat is admirable. Their mere presence in fashion is a step toward expanding the definition of beauty beyond a size six.

NOTES

1. Bordo 1993, p. 212.
2. For example, in Antebellum America, Sylvester Graham and other dietary reformers perceived excessive body weight as an indicator of moral failings. Intemperate and gluttonous behavior, which resulted in this excess of weight, illness, and even social disorder, could be remedied by abstinence from meat and starches, as prescribed by Graham. Salvation, via the stomach, was the ultimate goal of these dietary reformers of the 1830s. This concept of weight, with its moral implications, posited weight as an indicator of spiritual well-being. See Banner 1983; Gilman 2008; Schwartz 1986; Shryock 1966; Stearns 1997 for more on the history of the fat body.
3. See Czerniawski 2007, 2010 for a history of the creation of height and weight tables. Used originally as tools to facilitate the standardization of the medical selection process throughout the life insurance industry, these tables later operationalized the notion of ideal weight and became recommended guidelines for body weights. The height and weight table was transformed from a "tool of the trade" into a means of practicing social regulation. The popularization of this tool by medical, educational, and public institutions produced a new way of classifying bodies into underweight, overweight, and normal weight categories. With these guidelines established, Americans internalized a normalizing gaze and employed individualized disciplinary practices in order to conform their bodies to an established ideal. By tracing the history of the height and weight table, we see how weight guidelines serve to discipline populations by shifting public attention toward a body that needs to be measured and disciplined.
4. See Czerniawski 2007. Since the origins of these tables, physicians and actuaries have criticized their applicability to the general public. Before 1908, height and weight tables for women were not based on collected measurements but rather extrapolated from the men's table.
5. In recent years, scientists have debated the utility of BMI, given its inability to distinguish between the weight of muscle versus that of fat, e.g., under the current scale many Olympic athletes and professional football players would be classified as obese. Some studies even suggest that BMI standards need to be adjusted to account for racial and ethnic differences in body composition. An example of this can be found in Deurenberg et al. 1998.
6. See Popenoe 2005.

7. See Gross 2005.

8. Reported in Melago 2009.

9. Reported in Diluna 2010; Horne 2010.

10. Western culture did not always equate thinness with ideal beauty. In the 1860s, for example, a more voluptuous body challenged the fragile, thin idealized body of the antebellum era. This new curvaceous figure became the model of beauty, a reflection of health and vigor. By the 1870s, voluptuous women appeared in popular art, theaters, and across the various class sectors of society. Stage actresses, such as Lillian Russell, wore costumes with corsets that emphasized their round shape. This shift toward the idealization of a more curvy body coincided with a standardization of dress sizes due to the emergence of ready-to-wear apparel, drawing more attention to body shape. An 1899 article in the *Ladies Home Journal* described the perfect woman as one with weight proportionate to height: a height between five feet three inches and five feet seven inches, weighting between 125 and 140 pounds, bust measurement of twenty-eight to thirty-six inches, the hips about six to ten inches larger than the bust measurement, and a waist between twenty-two and twenty-eight inches. Retail drove a cultural preoccupation with body size and proportions. See Banner 1983; Gilman 2008; Schwartz 1986; Shryock 1966; Stearns 1997 for more on the history of idealized bodies.

11. Some of the models identified as fat while others as "normal" or "average."

12. Reported in Vesilind 2009.

13. Female fashion models are, on average, between fourteen and twenty-four years of age, at least five feet eight inches tall, and wear a size two through six, with measurements close to 34-24-34 inches. Typical runway models wear a size zero or size four, depending on each design season's aesthetics.

14. Some of the top-ranked modeling agencies will include the occasional size eight model on their plus-size roster. Generally, the models are from size ten to size eighteen, but most of the models in the top modeling agencies are size ten to size fourteen, alluding to a status system based on size. Plus-size models, similar to models in other divisions, face height requirements, as well. Models need to be a minimum height of five feet eight inches with a usual maximum of six feet tall.

15. There has been a change in the nomenclature for plus-size clothing, a subdivision of specialty retail, from "larger sizes" to "plus size." The labeling of clothing as plus size gained prominence in the 1990s, replacing the term "larger sizes."

16. See Hilbert et al. 2008; Puhl and Brownell 2001; Roehling 1999; Schwartz et al. 2006.

17. See Puhl and Brownell 2003.

18. See Schwartz et al. 2006.

19. See Schwartz et al. 2003.

20. To be clear, Goffman does not focus on the body per se but on the presentation of the self that is produced through interaction. He situates individuals in a social

context where the self is part of an interactive social project. See Goffman 1963a, p. 35; 1963b.

21. A stigmatized individual, as defined by Goffman, is tainted and possesses a failing or handicap that creates a discrepancy between the normative expectations or stereotypes concerning that individual (i.e., his/her *virtual* social identity) and the attributes and abilities the individual demonstrates to possess *in actu* (i.e., his/her *actual* social identity). See Goffman 1963b.

22. An individual then self-classifies as a "failed" member of society. These "vocabularies" are also used to self-classify the individual, wherein "if a person's bodily appearance and management categorizes them as a 'failed' member of society by others, they will internalize that label and incorporate it into what becomes a 'spoiled' self-identity." See Shilling 1993, p. 75.

23. For more on fat activism, see the work of Cooper 1998; Farrell 2011; Saguy and Ward 2010.

24. With bodies as mirrors of society, the bodies of plus-size models reflect the subjective tensions toward body weight and illuminate thinness as a master status. Their presence challenges the dominant valuation of the body as they present a desirable image of a plus-size woman that directly contrasts with the idealized thin feminine aesthetic. It is through their struggle to establish themselves as visible and marketable that we see how values are negotiated within a cultural discourse.

25. Bourdieu 1984, p. 190. For more on Bourdieu's theory on the role of bodily practices in class formation, see Bourdieu 2000, 2001.

26. Bourdieu 1984, p. 213.

27. Reported in Engel 2013.

28. See Pesa and Turner 1999.

29. See Piran, Levine, and Steiner-Adair 1999; Striegel-Moore and Smolak 2001.

30. Reported in Dolnick 2011.

31. For an explanation on the institutionalization of the white body as the preferred body in fashion, see Mears 2011.

32. See Burns-Ardolino 2009; Molina Guzman and Valdivia 2010.

33. Giovanelli and Ostertag 2009, p. 290.

34. Millman 1980, p. 202.

35. Blum 2003, p. 5.

36. While feminist scholarship has focused on the fat body as a site of resistance to patriarchal domination (see Bordo 1993; Braziel and LeBesco 2001; Chernin 1981; Hartley 2001; McKinley 1999; Orbach 1978; Rothblum and Solovay 2009) and others have focused on identity politics and social movements by studying the work of groups such as the National Organization to Advance Fat Acceptance (see Germov and Williams 1999; LeBesco 2001; Sobal 1999), the literature fails to acknowledge the role of plus-size models, as aesthetic laborers, in negotiating and manipulating cultural interpretations and expectations of women's bodies. See

Cooper 1998; LeBesco 2001; Levy-Navarro 2009; Solovay and Rothblum 2009; Wann 2009.

37. For studies of burlesque dancers, see Asbill 2009; McAllister 2009. For studies on theater performers, see Jester 2009; Kuppers 2001.

38. Asbill 2009, p. 300.

39. Murray 2005b, p. 161.

40. Ibid.

41. Baudrillard 2005, p. 278.

42. Wacquant 1995, p. 88.

43. To understand the modeling industry, I learned how to model, for "sociologists who want to understand meaning-making in everyday life have to observe and experience these embodied practices, as they unfold in real time and space, and materialize in real bodies. We, like the people we study, must learn the practices." See Eliasoph 2005, p. 160.

44. To maintain confidentiality, I changed names of people, places, and agencies when requested. To understand the decision made by those in charge of a model's career, I also interviewed eight modeling agents, four of whom were directors of plus-size divisions within their agencies, from four different agencies with offices in New York City. Some agents solicited for an interview chose not to participate in this study. Two of the agencies primarily dealt with fit and commercial print modeling, while the other two dealt exclusively with fashion print. The recruited agents participated in open-ended, semi-structured interviews conducted in their place of work that lasted approximately one hour. In an industry built on crafting images, merely interviewing the fashion tastemakers resulted in carefully constructed responses and colorful vignettes. I peeled back the many layers of these tales, in combination with my lived experience as a model, to understand the mechanisms guiding agency procedures and practices.

NOTES TO CHAPTER 2

1. The stigmatization of a fat woman based on a personal attribute and subsequent internalization and incorporation of this label is similar in process to labeling behavior as deviant in societal reaction theory. In societal reaction theory, deviance is a product of the interactive dynamic between individuals in a society. A deviant behavior is one that violates social norms. From this perspective, labeling an individual as a deviant is a process, which can ultimately lead to an internalization of a deviant label, i.e., Lemert's concept of secondary deviance. Secondary deviance alters an individual's self-concept and affects interactions with others such that it reinforces the deviant label and results in a continuation of the deviant behavior. For example, as a secondary deviant, a plus-size model takes on the label of "plus size" as a key aspect of her identity. Labeled as plus size, the model reinforces her deviant behaviors by fulfilling the role expectations of this new status. She needs to maintain her weight, which is the source of her stigmatization,

at all costs in order to work. In turn, the modeling industry promotes and reinforces her deviant behaviors—binging and overeating—through active and passive means of social control. A plus-size model endures her stigmatization and incorporates the "plus-size" label into her own identity while working within an institution that exploits her size. For more on deviance, see Becker 1964; Lemert 1951; Pfohl 1994.

2. Reported in 2006c.
3. For more on cultural producers and the aesthetic economy, see Entwistle 2002; Godart and Mears 2009; Mears 2008, 2010; Neff et al. 2005.
4. Reported in D'Innocenzio 1998.
5. Reported in Klepacki 1999.
6. Reported in Witchel 1997.
7. Reported in McCall 2013a.
8. Reported in Miller 2013.

NOTES TO CHAPTER 3

1. In August 2006, Ramos died of heart failure during a fashion show. She had been advised to lose weight and went days without eating or simply subsisting on lettuce and diet soda. Then in November of the same year, Reston died. She weighed forty kilograms at the time of death. Reported in 2006d; Taylor 2006.
2. Reported in Chernikoff 2011; Goldwert 2011; Yuan 2010.
3. Reported in Emery 2012.
4. Bernstein and St. John 2009, pp. 263–64.
5. Reported in Rochlin 2008.
6. Reported in Quinn 2008.
7. Reported in Sims 2002.
8. Ibid.
9. Reported in Weston 2008.
10. Reported in Quinn 2006.
11. Reported in Chernikoff 2013.
12. Reported in Cardellino 2013.

NOTES TO CHAPTER 4

1. Entwistle and Wissinger 2006, p. 777.
2. Hochschild 1983, p. 7; Wissinger 2004, p. x.
3. Wissinger 2004, p. 211.
4. Ibid., pp. 108–9.
5. Reported in Amador 2006.
6. For more on gender performativity, see Butler 1988.
7. For more on the social construction of gender, see West and Zimmerman 1987.
8. Foucault 1975, p. 138.
9. Wacquant 2004, p. 127.

10. Reported in Laurel 2008.
11. The standardization of dress sizes in ready-to-wear apparel started in the 1870s, but mostly focused on men's clothing. Due to greater variability of women's bodies, women's clothes continued to be custom-made until the 1920s. When clothing manufacturers did produce women's clothes, they often created their own unique sizing system that resulted in a lack of size consistency across the garment industry and generally poor fit that required at-home alterations. Therefore, the National Bureau of Home Economics of the U.S. Department of Agriculture conducted the first large-scale study of women's body measurements in 1937. The purpose of the study was to create a sizing system for the garment industry that reflected the measurements of women's bodies. In 1941, the results were published as USDA Miscellaneous Publication 454, Women's Measurements for Garment and Pattern Construction. Over the next decade, the USDA collected additional data and published updated guidelines, Commercial Standard (CS)215–58, in 1958. As the bodies of American men and women grew fatter, the standard size guidelines no longer reflected the size and shape of the population. The average woman's body, in particular, transformed from an hourglass shape to a pear shape. Since the 1980s, manufacturers have abandoned the use of these size guidelines and have begun selling bigger clothes labeled with smaller size numbers, i.e., vanity sizing. See National Institute of Standards and Technology 2004.
12. Reported in Bell 2011.

NOTES TO CHAPTER 5
1. Crossley 2001, p. 107.
2. For more on the concept of habitus, see Bourdieu 1984.
3. Mears 2011, pp. 123–24.
4. Ibid., p. 125.
5. Agencies often write off the debts of "failed models," i.e., those who do not earn enough to recoup expenses, as a business expense. For more on the economics of the agency system, sees Mears 2011, pp. 59–68.
6. See Dean 2003, 2005, 2013.
7. Crossley 2004, pp. 40–41.
8. Mears 2011, pp. 72–73, 198.
9. This is in sharp contrast to film and television performers, who are represented by the Screen Actors Guild (SAG), as well as Actors' Equity, which represents theatrical actors and stage managers.
10. Reported in 2008.
11. Reported in Sauers 2010.
12. Reported in 2009.
13. See Eaton, Lowry, et al. 2005; Crosnoe 2007 for examples of this connection between body weight and suicide.
14. Munster 2013.

15. Reported in Conti 2007.
16. Reported in Adams 2013. For more on the union's benefits for models, see http://www.equity.org.uk/models/.
17. Reported in Lehman 2012.
18. Ibid.
19. See http://modelalliance.org/mission.

NOTES TO CHAPTER 6

1. An exposé article published in *The New Yorker* later disputed this claim. See Collins 2008.
2. See Stevenson 2005.
3. Reported in 2010; Shaw 2010.
4. Reported in Monget 1999.
5. Reported in Greenberg 2006.
6. Reported in Burling 2006.
7. Reported in 2006a; Greenberg 2006.
8. Reported in Burling 2006.
9. Reported in Monget 2006.
10. See 2004b.
11. Reported in Kovanis 2006. See Lane Bryant's corporate website at http://www.ascenaretail.com/lanebryant.jsp.
12. See Cohen 2013.
13. Reported in Gogoi 2006; Kovanis 2006; Mikus 2006; Yao 2006.
14. Reported in Li 2012.
15. Ibid.
16. Ibid.; Yao 2006.
17. Reported in Chandler 2006.
18. Reported in Li 2012.
19. Reported in Mikus 2006.
20. Reported in Li 2012.
21. Reported in Amador 2006.
22. Reported in Seckler 2003.
23. Reported in 2004a.
24. Reported in Seckler 2003.
25. Reported in Sarkisian-Miller 2006.
26. Reported in Denizet-Lewis 2006.
27. Reported in Guo 2013.
28. Reported in Daswani 2004.
29. Reported in Li 2012.
30. Reported in Yadegaran McClatchy 2006.
31. Reported in Bloomfield 1989a, 1989b.
32. Reported in Bloomfield 1989a.

33. Reported in D'Innocenzio 1992.
34. Reported in Krupnick 2013.
35. Reported in Simon 1995.
36. Reported in D'Innocenzio 1997.
37. Reported in D'Innocenzio 1994.
38. Reported in Fung 2000.
39. Ibid.
40. Reported in Lee 1998.
41. Ibid.
42. Reported in Wilson 1997.
43. Reported in Simon 1995.
44. Reported in Amador 2007.
45. Reported in Jones 2007.
46. Reported in Sarkisian-Miller 2006.
47. Reported in Li 2012.
48. Reported in Simon 1995.
49. Reported in Greenberg 2005.
50. Reported in Li 2012.
51. Reported in McCall 2013b.
52. Reported in Black 2013.
53. See http://www.luscious-plus-lingerie.com/aboutus.sc.
54. Gruys 2012, p. 487.
55. Ibid., p. 494.
56. See Contrino 2007a, 2007b; Diadul 2007.
57. See http://www.hipsandcurves.com/about-us.
58. See Hips and Curves 2006, 2009.
59. See http://www.curvycouture.com.
60. See http://www.luscious-plus-lingerie.com/aboutus.sc.
61. Murray 2005b, p. 161.

NOTES TO CHAPTER 7

1. Blum 2003, p. 101.
2. See Bakhtin 2005.
3. Baudrillard 2005, pp. 278–79.
4. Ibid., p. 278.
5. This commercial persona of the plus-size woman is "a construction that performs the cultural work of personifying a market relation by giving a face and personality to a market category," in other words, the consumer in the abstract. See Cook 2004; Cook and Kaiser 2004, p. 209.
6. Crossley 2004, pp. 40–41.
7. Goffman 1963b, p. 115.

8. Models inhabit the extremes in weight distribution—the ultra-skinny and the fat. Both a runway and plus-size model are strategically deviant. While a high-fashion runway model is deviant because of her extreme thinness and propensity to engage in disordered eating behaviors, she is generally not stigmatized because thinness is a master status. She stands out for her lack of fat, while the plus-size model stands out because of her fat.
9. Reported in Jones 2006.
10. Reported in 2006b.
11. Reported in 2007; Heckle 2007.
12. Reported in Johnson 2007.
13. Reported in Wilson 2012.
14. Reported in Olins 2008.
15. Reported in Figueroa-Jones 2007.
16. See Hamilton et al. 2007; Kilbourne 1999; Knauss et al. 2008; Wolf 1992.
17. Their work is no different from any other model of any size in fashion. All models must control and discipline their bodies.

REFERENCES

2004a. "Lagerfeld's High Street Split." *Vogue*, November 18, 2004, http://www.vogue.co.uk/news/2004/11/18/lagerfelds-high-street-split. Accessed March 5, 2013.

2004b. "Lane Bryant, Inc." *International Directory of Company Histories*, http://www.fundinguniverse.com/company-histories/Lane-Bryant-Inc-Company-History.html. Accessed August 2, 2008.

2006a. "As Bustlines Expand, 1st Plus-Size-Only Lingerie Store Opens: Plus-Size Women Now Have a Lingerie Boutique All Their Own." June 12, 2006, http://www.ereleases.com/pr/as-bustlines-expand-1st-plussizeonly-lingerie-store-opens-7571. Accessed March 5, 2013.

2006b. "Brazil Model Who Battled Anorexia Dies." *Washington Post*, November 16, 2006, http://www.washingtonpost.com/wp-dyn/content/article/2006/11/16/AR2006111601392.html. Accessed March 15, 2013.

2006c. "Plus-Size Model Crystal Renn Speaks About Overcoming Anorexia to Become a Plus-Size Model." NBC News Transcripts, September 4, 2006, LexisNexis Academic. Web. Accessed February 12, 2013.

2006d. "Where Size 0 Doesn't Make the Cut." *New York Times*, September 22, 2006, http://www.nytimes.com/2006/09/22/opinion/22fri4.html?_r=0. Accessed October 23, 2013.

2007. "Spain Bans Skinny Sizes on Mannequins." Associated Press, March 13, 2007, http://www.nbcnews.com/id/17596139/#.UUPTqa7ry4I. Accessed March 15, 2013.

2008. "Ruslana Korshunova, Supermodel, Dies In Fall." *Huffington Post*, June 28, 2008, http://www.huffingtonpost.com/2008/06/28/ruslana-korshunova-superm_n_109792.html. Accessed November 26, 2013.

2009. "Daul Kim Dead: 20-Year-Old Model Found Hanged In Paris Apartment." *Huffington Post*, November 20, 2009, http://www.huffingtonpost.com/2009/11/20/daul-kim-dead-20-year-old_n_364350.html. Accessed November 27, 2013.

2010. "Lingerie Ads Nixed Due to Plus-Sized Model?" CBS News, April 26, 2010, http://www.cbsnews.com/2100-3480_162-6428418.html. Accessed March 5, 2013.

Adams, Rebecca. 2013. "Equity Model Code of Conduct Signed By British *Vogue*." *Huffington Post*, April 9, 2013, http://www.huffingtonpost.com/2013/04/09/equity-model-code-of-conduct-british-vogue_n_3045688.html. Accessed November 27, 2013.

Amador, Valery. 2006. "Plus Model Magazine Launches 2nd Issue with Curvy Cover Model Angellika." *PLUS Model Magazine*, September 1, 2006, http://www.

plus-model-mag.com/2006/09/plus-model-magazine-launches-2nd-issue-with-curvy-cover-model-angellika/. Accessed February 12, 2013.

———. 2007. "Cherished Woman Offers Stylish Plus Size Clothing." *PLUS Model Magazine*, March 1, 2007, http://www.plusmodelmag.com/General/plus-model-magazine-article-detail.asp?article-id=704723368. Accessed March 5, 2013.

Asbill, D. Lacy. 2009. ""I'm Allowed to Be a Sexual Being": The Distinctive Social Conditions of the Fat Burlesque Stage." In *The Fat Studies Reader*, edited by Esther Rothblum and Sondra Solovay, 299–304. New York: New York University Press.

Bakhtin, Mikhail. 2005. "The Grotesque Image of the Body and Its Sources." In *The Body: A Reader*, edited by Mariam Fraser and Monica Greco, 92–95. London; New York: Routledge.

Banner, Lois W. 1983. *American Beauty*. New York: Knopf, Distributed by Random House.

Bartky, Sandra. 1988. "Foucault, Femininity and the Modernization of Patriarchal Power." In *Feminism and Foucault: Paths of Resistance*, edited by Lee Quinby and Irene Diamond, 61–86. Boston: Northeastern University Press.

Baudrillard, Jean. 2005. "The Finest Consumer Object." In *The Body: A Reader*, edited by Mariam Fraser and Monica Greco, 277–82. London; New York: Routledge.

Becker, Anne E. 1995. *Body, Self, and Society: The View from Fiji*. Philadelphia: University of Pennsylvania Press.

Becker, Howard Saul. 1964. *The Other Side: Perspectives on Deviance*. New York: Free Press.

Bell, Crystal. 2011. "'Big Sexy' Exclusive Interview: Cast of TLC's 'Big Sexy' Talk Being Plus-Sized in a Skinny Girl's Fashion World." *Huffington Post*, September 13, 2011, http://www.huffingtonpost.com/2011/09/13/big-sexy-exclusive-interview-tlc_n_960861.html. Accessed November 12, 2011.

Bernstein, Beth and Matilda St. John. 2009. "The Roseanne Benedict Arnolds: How Fat Women Are Betrayed by Their Celebrity Icons." In *The Fat Studies Reader*, edited by Esther Rothblum and Sondra Solovay, 263–70. New York: New York University Press.

Black, Liz. 2013. "Meet The First Plus-Size Designer To Show At NYFW." *Refinery29*, August 31, 2013, http://www.refinery29.com/2013/08/52328/cabiria-plus-size-show-nyfw#page-1. Accessed January 10, 2014.

Bloomfield, Judy. 1989a. "Plus Size Designers Group Created." *Women's Wear Daily* 158, 21: 13.

———. 1989b. "Plus Size Show Launched to 250 at Bloomingdale's." *Women's Wear Daily* 158, 50: 36.

Blum, Virginia L. 2003. *Flesh Wounds: The Culture of Cosmetic Surgery*. Berkeley: University of California Press.

Bordo, Susan. 1993. *Unbearable Weight: Feminism, Western Culture, and the Body*. Berkeley: University of California Press.

Bourdieu, Pierre. 1984. *Distinction: A Social Critique of the Judgment of Taste*. Cambridge, MA: Harvard University Press.

———. 2000. *Pascalian Meditations*. Stanford, CA: Stanford University Press.

———. 2001. *Masculine Domination*. Stanford, CA: Stanford University Press.

Braziel, Jana Evans and Kathleen LeBesco. 2001. *Bodies Out of Bounds: Fatness and Transgression*. Berkeley: University of California Press.

Brumberg, Joan Jacobs. 1997. *The Body Project: An Intimate History of American Girls*. New York: Random House.

Budgeon, Shelley. 2003. "Identity as an Embodied Event." *Body & Society* 9: 35–55.

Burling, Stacey. 2006. "Risque Business: New Lane Bryant Store at King of Prussia Mall." *Philadelphia Inquirer*, October 22, 2006, http://www.highbeam.com/doc/1G1-153158640.html. Accessed March 5, 2013.

Burns-Ardolino, Wendy A. 2009. "Jiggle in My Walk: The Iconic Power of the "Big Butt" in American Pop Culture." In *The Fat Studies Reader*, edited by Esther Rothblum and Sondra Solovay, 271–79. New York: New York University Press.

Butler, Judith. 1988. "Performative Acts and Gender Constitution: An Essay in Phenomenology and Feminist Theory." *Theatre Journal* 40, 4: 519–31.

Cardellino, Carly. 2013. "World's Top Modeling Agency Now Casting Talent Regardless of Size, Race, and Age." *Cosmopolitan*, November 17, 2013, http://www.cosmopolitan.com/celebrity/news/img-models-integrates-all-talent. Accessed November 23, 2013.

Chandler, Susan. 2006. "Retailers Are Sizing Up an Overlooked Market: Department Stores and Boutiques Devote More Choices, Attention to Plus-Size Shoppers." *Chicago Tribune*, May 28, 2006, http://articles.chicagotribune.com/2006-05-28/business/0605280036_1_plus-size-market-larger-sizes-retailers/. Accessed March 5, 2013.

Chernikoff, Leah. 2011. "Crystal Renn Is Not a Size Two Despite What Her Ford Model Card Says." *Fashionista*, January 31, 2011, http://fashionista.com/2011/01/crystal-renn-is-not-a-size-two-despite-what-her-ford-model-card-says/. Accessed February 11, 2013.

———. 2013. "First Modeling Agency Devoted to Girls of All Sizes Sets Up Shop in NYC." *Fashionista*, July, 18, 2013, http://fashionista.com/2013/07/first-modeling-agency-devoted-to-girls-of-all-sizes-sets-up-shop-in-nyc/. Accessed November 2, 2013.

Chernin, Kim. 1981. *The Obsession: Reflections on the Tyranny of Slenderness*. New York: Harper & Row.

Cohen, Marshal. 2013. "Put a Fork In It. Signs The Recession Is Finally Behind Us." NPD Group Blog, July 11, 2013, https://www.npdgroupblog.com/put-a-fork-in-it-signs-the-recession-is-finally-behind-us/#.UredUPZtlhA. Accessed December 22, 2013.

Collins, Lauren. 2008. "Pixel Perfect: Pascal Dangin's Virtual Reality." *New Yorker*, May 12, 2008, http://www.newyorker.com/reporting/2008/05/12/080512fa_fact_collins. Accessed June 2, 2008.

Conti, Samantha. 2007. "British Models Join Actors' Equity Union." *Women's Wear Daily*, December 11, 2007, http://www.wwd.com/fashion-news/fashion-features/british-models-join-actors-equity-union-473813. Accessed November 27, 2013.

Contrino, Tom. 2007a. "Midnight Magic." United Retail Incorporated, http://www.avenue.com. Accessed December 9, 2008.

———. 2007b. "Moonlit Moments." United Retail Incorporated, http://www.avenue.com. Accessed December 9, 2008.

Cook, Daniel Thomas. 2004. *The Commodification of Childhood: The Children's Clothing Industry and the Rise of the Child Consumer*. Durham, NC: Duke University Press.

Cook, Daniel Thomas and Susan B. Kaiser. 2004. "Betwixt and Be Tween: Age Ambiguity and the Sexualization of the Female Consuming Subject." *Journal of Consumer Culture* 4: 203–27.

Cooper, Charlotte. 1998. *Fat and Proud: The Politics of Size*. London: Women's Press.

Crosnoe, Robert. 2007. "Gender, Obesity, and Education." *Sociology of Education* 80, 3: 241–60.

Crossley, Nick. 2001. *The Social Body: Habit, Identity and Desire*. London: Sage.

———. 2004. "The Circuit Trainer's Habitus: Reflexive Body Techniques and the Sociality of the Workout." *Body & Society* 10, 1: 37–69.

Czerniawski, Amanda M. 2007. "From Average to Ideal: The Evolution of the Height and Weight Table in the United States, 1836–1943." *Social Science History* 31, 2: 273–96.

———. 2010. "Commentary: Symonds' Curious Fat Fact." *International Journal of Epidemiology* 39: 959–63.

———. 2012. "Disciplining Corpulence: The Case of Plus-Size Fashion Models." *Journal of Contemporary Ethnography* 41, 2: 3–29.

Daswani, Kavita. 2004. "A Growing Market: After Adding Up the Benefits, Specialty Retailers Are Expanding into the Plus-Size Category." *Women's Wear Daily*, September 29: 72S.

Davis, Kathy. 1995. *Reshaping the Female Body: The Dilemma of Cosmetic Surgery*. New York: Routledge.

Dean, Deborah. 2003. "If Women Actors Were Working . . . " *Media, Culture & Society* 25: 527–41.

———. 2005. "Recruiting a Self: Women Performers and Aesthetic Labour." *Work, Employment and Society* 19, 4: 761–74.

———. 2013. *Performing Ourselves: Actors, Social Stratification and Work*. Basingstoke: Palgrave Macmillan.

Denizet-Lewis, Benoit. 2006. "The Man behind Abercrombie & Fitch." *Salon*, January 24, 2006, http://www.salon.com/2006/01/24/jeffries/. Accessed December 22, 2013.

Deurenberg, P., M. Yap, and W. A. Van Staveren. 1998. "Body Mass Index and Percent Body Fat: A Meta Analysis Among Different Ethnic Groups." *International Journal of Obesity and Related Metabolic Disorders* 22, 12: 1164–71.

Diadul, Robert. 2007. "Wild Nights." United Retail Incorporated, http://www.avenue.com. Accessed December 9, 2008.

Diluna, Amy. 2010. "Sick World Where Size 4 Is Too Fat." *Daily News*, February 16, 2010, http://www.nydailynews.com/life-style/fashion/size-4-fashion-week-model-coco-rocha-21-latest-women-considered-fat-industry-article-1.195616. Accessed January 5, 2011.

D'Innocenzio, Anne. 1992. "Emphasis on Super-Sizes, Merger Boost Catherines' Plus-Size Share." *Women's Wear Daily*, October 28, 1992: 30.

———. 1994. "Pursuing a Fashion Customer." *Women's Wear Daily*, October 6, 1994: 8.

———. 1997. "A New Attitude: Plus-Size Pride." *Women's Wear Daily*, August 20, 1997: 10.

———. 1998. "Emme: A Model of Self-Esteem." *Women's Wear Daily*, March 5, 1998: 9.

Dolnick, Sam. 2011. "Ethnic Differences Emerge in Plastic Surgery." *New York Times*, February 18, 2011, http://www.nytimes.com/2011/02/19/nyregion/19plastic.html?pagewanted=all&_r=0. Accessed February 19, 2011.

Douglas, Mary. 2005. "The Two Bodies." In *The Body: A Reader*, edited by Mariam Fraser and Monica Greco, 78–81. London; New York: Routledge.

Eaton, D. K., R. Lowry, et al. 2005. "Associations of Body Mass Index and Perceived Weight with Suicide Ideation and Suicide Attempts Among US High School Students." *Archives of Pediatrics and Adolescent Medicine* 159, 6: 513–19.

Eliasoph, Nina. 2005. "Theorizing from the Neck Down: Why Social Research Must Understand Bodies Acting in Real Space and Time (and Why It's So Hard to Spell Out What We Learn from This)." *Qualitative Sociology* 28, 2: 159–69.

Emery, Debbie. 2012. "Plus Size Women Feel 'Betrayed and Insulted' by Crystal Renn's Startling Slimdown." Radaronline.com, January 30, 2012, http://www.radaronline.com/exclusives/2012/01/crystal-renn-s-startling-slimdown-plus-size-women-betrayed. Accessed February 11, 2013.

Engel, Pamela. 2013. "Women in a Poor West African Country Are Force-Feeding Themselves for Beauty's Sake." Businessinsider.com, May 23, 2013, http://www.businessinsider.com/women-force-feeding-in-mauritania-2013-5?op=1#ixzz2ezMG6Vb5. Accessed September 15, 2013.

Entwistle, Joanne. 2002. "The Aesthetic Economy: The Production of Value in the Field of Fashion Modelling." *Journal of Consumer Culture* 2, 3: 317–39.

Entwistle, Joanne and Elizabeth Wissinger. 2006. "Keeping Up Appearances: Aesthetic Labour in the Fashion Modelling Industries of London and New York." *Sociological Review* 54, 4: 774–94.

Farrell, Amy Erdman. 2011. *Fat Shame: Stigma and the Fat Body in American Culture*. New York: New York University Press.

Figueroa-Jones, Maddy. 2007. "Velvet D'amour Opens Up on Her Curvy Life and Controversies." *PLUS Model Magazine*, March 1, 2007, http://www.plusmodelmag.com/General/plus-model-magazine-article-detail.asp?article-id=404880624. Accessed March 15, 2013.

Foucault, Michel. 1975. *Discipline and Punish: The Birth of the Prison*. New York: Vintage Books.

Frost, Liz. 2005. "Theorizing the Young Woman in the Body." *Body & Society* 11, 1: 63–85.

Fung, Shirley. 2000. "Plus Sizes: A Largely Untapped Area." *Women's Wear Daily*, September 20, 2000: 18.

Geertz, Clifford. 1988. *Works and Lives: The Anthropologist as Author*. Stanford, CA: Stanford University Press.

Germov, John and Lauren Williams. 1999. "Dieting Women: Self-Surveillance and the Body Panopticon." In *Weighty Issues: Fatness and Thinness as Social Problems*, edited by Jeffery Sobal and Donna Maurer, 117–32. Hawthorne, NY: Aldine de Gruyter.

Giddens, Anthony. 1991. *Modernity and Self-Identity: Self and Society in the Late Modern Age*. Stanford, CA: Stanford University Press.

Gilman, Sander L. 2008. *Fat: A Cultural History of Obesity*. Cambridge, UK; Malden, MA: Polity.

Giovanelli, Dina and Stephen Ostertag. 2009. "Controlling the Body: Media Representations, Body Size, and Self-Discipline." In *The Fat Studies Reader*, edited by Esther Rothblum and Sondra Solovay, 289–96. New York: New York University Press.

Godart, Frederic C. and Ashley Mears. 2009. "How Do Cultural Producers Make Creative Decisions? Lessons from the Catwalk." *Social Forces* 88, 2: 671–92.

Goffman, Erving. 1959. *The Presentation of Self in Everyday Life*. Garden City, NY: Doubleday.

———. 1963a. *Behavior in Public Places: Notes on the Social Organization of Gatherings*. New York: Free Press of Glencoe.

———. 1963b. *Stigma: Notes on the Management of Spoiled Identity*. Englewood Cliffs, NJ: Prentice-Hall.

———. 1967. *Interaction Ritual: Essays on Face-to-Face Behavior*. New York: Pantheon Books.

———. 2005 [1963]. "Embodied Information in Face-to-Face Interaction." In *The Body: A Reader*, edited by Mariam Fraser and Monica Greco, 82–86. London; New York: Routledge.

Gogoi, Pallavi. 2006. "The Skinny on Plus-Size Apparel." *BusinessWeek* Online, March 24, 2006, http://www.businessweek.com/bwdaily/dnflash/mar2006/nf20060324_6779_db016.htm. Accessed June 1, 2006.

Goldwert, Lindsay. 2011. "Crystal Renn Slams 'Plus Size' Controversy; Sez She'd Have 'Binge Eating Disorder' to Be 'Plus Size.'" *Daily News*, February 16, 2011, http://articles.nydailynews.com/2011-02-16/entertainment/28622242_1_straight-size-model-crystal-renn-straight-size. Accessed January 5, 2012.

Greenberg, Julee. 2005. "Igigi's Plus-Size Fashion Formula." *Women's Wear Daily*, June 15, 2005: 10.

———. 2006. "Lane Bryant Plans New Lingerie Stores." *Women's Wear Daily* 192, March 13, 2006: 4.

Gross, Joan. 2005. "Phat." In *Fat: The Anthropology of an Obsession*, edited by Don Kulick and Anne Meneley, 63–76. New York: Jeremy P. Tarcher/Penguin.

Gruys, Kjerstin. 2012. "Does This Make Me Look Fat? Aesthetic Labor and Fat Talk as Emotional Labor in a Women's Plus-Size Clothing Store." *Social Problems* 59, 4: 481–500.

Guo, Jia. 2013. "Abercrombie & Fitch to Offer Plus-Sizes." *CNN Money*, November 20, 2013, http://money.cnn.com/2013/11/20/investing/abercrombie-fitch-plus-sizes/. Accessed December 22, 2013.

Hamilton, Emily, Laurie Mintz, et al. 2007. "Predictors of Media Effects on Body Dissatisfaction in European American Women." *Sex Roles* 56, 5/6: 397–402.

Hartley, Cecilia. 2001. "Letting Ourselves Go: Making Room for the Fat Body in Feminist Scholarship." In *Bodies Out of Bounds: Fatness and Transgression*, edited by Jana Evans Braziel and Kathleen LeBesco, 60–73. Berkeley and Los Angeles: University of California Press.

Heckle, Harold. 2007. "Top Spanish Fashion Show Rejects 5 Women." *Washington Post*, February 11, 2007, http://www.washingtonpost.com/wp-dyn/content/article/2007/02/11/AR2007021100658.html. Accessed March 15, 2013.

Hilbert, Anja, Winfried Rief, et al. 2008. "Stigmatizing Attitudes toward Obesity in a Representative Population-Based Sample." *Obesity* 16, 7: 1529–34.

Hips and Curves. 2006. "Corsets & Bustiers." http://www.hipsandcurves.com. Accessed December 3, 2006.

———. 2009. "Lingerie for Women with Curves." http://www.hipsandcurves.com. Accessed February 2, 2009.

Hirsch, Paul M. 1972. "Processing Fads and Fashions: An Organization-Set Analysis of Cultural Industry Systems." *American Journal of Sociology* 77, 4: 639–59.

Hochschild, Arlie Russell. 1983. *The Managed Heart: Commercialization of Human Feeling*. Berkeley: University of California Press.

Horne, Sarah. 2010. "Gemma Ward, a Supermodel Betrayed." *Page Six Magazine*, February 11, 2010, http://www.nypost.com/pagesixmag/issues/20100211/Gemma+Ward+Supermodel+Betrayed#axzz2KYUOoPwW. Accessed January 5, 2011.

Jester, Julia Grace. 2009. "Placing Fat Women on Center Stage." In *The Fat Studies Reader*, edited by Esther Rothblum and Sondra Solovay, 249–55. New York: New York University Press.

Johnson, Mark. 2007. "New York Lawmaker Wants Model Weight Rules." *Washington Post*, January 31, 2007, http://www.washingtonpost.com/wp-dyn/content/article/2007/01/31/AR2007013100227.html. Accessed March 15, 2013.

Jones, Madeline. 2006. "Skinny Models: Delving into the Weight Debate." *PLUS Model Magazine*, November 1, 2006, http://www.plus-model-mag.com/2006/11/skinny-models-delving-into-the-weight-debate/. Accessed March 15, 2013.

———. 2007. "Fashion Frustrations Turned into Big Business for Plus-Size Designer, Jessica Svoboda." *PLUS Model Magazine*, January 12, 2007, http://www.plus-model-mag.com/2007/01/

fashion-frustrations-turned-into-big-business-for-plus-size-designer-jessica-svo-boda/. Accessed March 5, 2013.

Kilbourne, Jean. 1999. *Deadly Persuasion: Why Women and Girls Must Fight the Addictive Power of Advertising*. New York: Free Press.

Klepacki, Laura. 1999. "Emme: From Plus-Size Model to Role Model." *Women's Wear Daily*, August 13, 1999: 9.

Knauss, Christine, Susan J. Paxton, et al. 2008. "Body Dissatisfaction in Adolescent Boys and Girls: Objectified Body Consciousness, Internalization of the Media Body Ideal and Perceived Pressure from Media." *Sex Roles* 59, 9–10: 633–44.

Kovanis, Georgea. 2006. "Plus Size Gets Bigger." *Detroit Free Press*, June 26, 2006, http://www.accessmylibrary.com/article-1G1-147532014/plus-size-gets-bigger.html. Accessed March 5, 2013.

Krupnick, Ellie. 2013. "Tim Gunn: Fashion Seems to End at a Size 12." *Huffington Post*, August 23, 2013, http://www.huffingtonpost.com/2013/08/23/tim-gunn-size_n_3799450.html. Accessed December 23, 2013.

Kulick, Don and Anne Meneley. 2005. *Fat: The Anthropology of an Obsession*. New York: Jeremy P. Tarcher/Penguin.

Kuppers, Petra. 2001. "Fatties on Stage: Feminist Performances." In *Bodies Out of Bounds: Fatness and Transgression*, edited by Jana Evans Braziel and Kathleen LeBesco, 277–91. Berkeley and Los Angeles: University of California Press.

Laurel, Larissa. 2008. "Physical Requirements for Plus Models." *PLUS Model Magazine*, June 1, 2008, http://www.plusmodelmag.com/general/plus-model-magazine-article-detail.asp?article-id=811644543&page=0. Accessed June 1, 2008.

LeBesco, Kathleen. 2001. "Queering Fat Bodies/Politics." In *Bodies Out of Bounds: Fatness and Transgression*, edited by Jana Evans Braziel and Kathleen LeBesco, 74–87. Berkeley and Los Angeles: University of California Press.

Lee, Georgia. 1998. "Lane Bryant's V Team." *Women's Wear Daily*, July 15, 1998: 30.

Lehman, Daniel. 2012. "Supermodel Sara Ziff Starts Labor Movement with the Model Alliance." Backstage.com, February 6, 2012, http://www.backstage.com/news/supermodel-sara-ziff-starts-labor-movement-with-the-model-alliance/. Accessed November 27, 2013.

Lemert, Edwin McCarthy. 1951. *Social Pathology: A Systematic Approach to the Theory of Sociopathic Behavior*. New York: McGraw-Hill.

Levy-Navarro, Elena. 2009. "Fattening Queer History: Where Does Fat History Go from Here?" In *The Fat Studies Reader*, edited by Esther Rothblum and Sondra Solovay, 15–22. New York: New York University Press.

Li, Shan. 2012. "Clothing Lines Embrace Plus-Size Fashions." *Los Angeles Times*, August 26, 2012, http://articles.latimes.com/2012/aug/26/business/la-fi-plus-size-fashion-boom-20120826. Accessed December 16, 2012.

Lorber, Judith. 1994. ""Night to His Day": The Social Construction of Gender." In *Paradoxes of Gender*, 13–36. New Haven, CT: Yale University Press.

McAllister, Heather. 2009. "Embodying Fat Liberation." In *The Fat Studies Reader*, edited by Esther Rothblum and Sondra Solovay, 305–11. New York: New York University Press.

McCall, Tyler. 2013a. "Eden Miller Makes History as the First Designer to Show Plus-Size Line at Fashion Week." Fashionista.com, September 7, 2013, http://fashionista.com/2013/09/eden-miller-makes-history-as-the-first-designer-to-show-plus-size-line-at-fashion-week/. Accessed December 23, 2013.

———. 2013b. "Eden Miller to Show First Plus Size Line at New York Fashion Week." Fashionista.com, August 27, 2013, http://fashionista.com/2013/08/meet-eden-miller-the-designer-behind-the-first-plus-size-line-to-show-at-new-york-fashion-week/. Accessed January 9, 2014.

McKinley, Nita Mary. 1999. "Ideal Weight/Ideal Woman: Society Constructs the Female." In *Weighty Issues: Constructing Fatness and Thinness as Social Problems*, edited by Jeffery Sobal and Donna Maurer, 97–115. Hawthorne, NY: Aldine de Gruyter.

Mears, Ashley. 2008. "Discipline of the Catwalk: Gender, Power and Uncertainty in Fashion Modeling." *Ethnography* 9, 4: 429–56.

———. 2010. "Size Zero High-End Ethnic: Cultural Production and the Reproduction of Culture in Fashion Modeling." *Poetics* 38: 21–46.

———. 2011. *Pricing Beauty: The Making of a Fashion Model*. Berkeley and Los Angeles: University of California Press.

Mears, Ashley and William Finlay. 2005. "Not Just a Paper Doll: How Models Manage Bodily Capital and Why They Perform Emotional Labor." *Journal of Contemporary Ethnography* 34, 3: 317–43.

Melago, Carrie. 2009. "Ralph Lauren Model Filippa Hamilton: I Was Fired Because I Was Too Fat!" *Daily News*, October 14, 2009, http://www.nydailynews.com/life-style/fashion/ralph-lauren-model-filippa-hamilton-fired-fat-article-1.381093. Accessed January 5, 2011.

Mikus, Kim. 2006. "Torrid Sizes Up a Youth Movement." *Chicago Daily Herald*, May 21, 2006, http://www.highbeam.com/doc/1G1-146278403.html. Accessed March 5, 2013.

Miller, Tracy. 2013. "Plus-Size Models Strut Their Stuff at Pulp Fashion Week in Paris." *New York Daily News*, October 29, 2013, http://www.nydailynews.com/life-style/plus-size-models-strut-stuff-pulp-fashion-week-paris-article-1.1500019#ixzz2oMcYDyJ5. Accessed December 23, 2013.

Millman, Marcia. 1980. *Such a Pretty Face: Being Fat in America*. New York: Norton.

Molina Guzman, Isabel and Angharad N. Valdivia. 2010. "Brain, Brow, and Booty: Latina Iconicity in U.S. Popular Culture." In *The Politics of Women's Bodies: Sexuality, Appearance, and Behavior*, edited by Rose Weitz, 155–62. New York: Oxford University Press.

Monget, Karyn. 1999. "Sexy Intimates Bow at Lane Bryant." *Women's Wear Daily* 185, December 13, 1999: 14.

———. 2006. "Sexy, Luxe Lingerie Lifts Sales." *Women's Wear Daily* 192, 115: 8.

Munster, Tess. 2013. "The Dark Side of Modeling: What I Learned as a Plus Size Model." *Huffington Post*, August 21, 2013, http://www.huffingtonpost.com/tess-munster/dark-side-of-modeling_b_3787381.html. Accessed November 27, 2003.

Murphy, Alexandra G. 2003. "The Dialectical Gaze: Exploring the Subject-Object Tension in the Performances of Women Who Strip." *Journal of Contemporary Ethnography* 32, 3: 305–35.

Murray, Samantha. 2005a. "Doing Politics or Selling Out? Living the Fat Body." *Women's Studies: An Inter-Disciplinary Journal* 34, 3: 265–77.

———. 2005b. "(Un/Be)Coming Out? Rethinking Fat Politics." *Social Semiotics* 15, 2: 153–63.

National Institute of Standards and Technology. 2004. "Standardization of Women's Clothing." http://museum.nist.gov/exhibits/apparel/index.htm. Accessed November 10, 2013.

Neff, Gina, Elizabeth Wissinger, et al. 2005. "Entrepreneurial Labor among Cultural Producers: 'Cool' Jobs in 'Hot' Industries." *Social Semiotics* 15, 3: 307–34.

Olins, Alice. 2008. "Fashion Capitals End London's Plan to Ban Size Zero." *The Times*, August 13, 2008, http://women.timesonline.co.uk/tol/life_and_style/women/fashion/article4518268.ece. Accessed December 15, 2008.

Orbach, Susie. 1978. *Fat Is a Feminist Issue: The Anti-Diet Guide to Permanent Weight Loss*. New York: Paddington Press.

Pesa, Jacqueline A. and Lori W. Turner. 1999. "Ethnic and Racial Differences in Weight-Loss Behaviors among Female Adolescents: Results from a National Survey." *American Journal of Health Studies* 15: 14–21.

Pfohl, Stephen J. 1994. *Images of Deviance and Social Control: A Sociological History*. New York: McGraw-Hill.

Piran, Niva, Michael P. Levine, and Catherine Steiner-Adair. 1999. "The Looking Good, Feeling Good Program: A Multi-Ethnic Intervention for Healthy Image, Nutrition, and Physical Activity." In *Preventing Eating Disorders: A Handbook of Interventions and Special Challenges*, 175–93. Philadelphia, PA: Brunner/Mazel.

Popenoe, Rebecca. 2005. "Ideal." In *Fat: The Anthropology of an Obsession*, edited by Don Kulick and Anne Meneley, 9–28. New York: Jeremy P. Tarcher/Penguin.

Puhl, Rebecca M. and Kelly D. Brownell. 2001. "Bias, Discrimination, and Obesity." *Obesity Research* 9, 12: 788–805.

———. 2003. "Psychosocial Origins of Obesity Stigma: Toward Changing a Powerful and Pervasive Bias." *Obesity Reviews* 4: 213–27.

Quinn, Sharon. 2006. "Is a Size 12–14 a Plus Size????" Sharon Quinn: The Original Runway Diva Blogspot, http://therunwaydivasays.blogspot.com/2006_09_01_archive.html. Accessed July 3, 2008.

———. 2008. "'Model' Behavior: – Taking Your Career Seriously (the Business of You)." *PLUS Model Magazine*, May 1, 2008, http://www.plusmodelmag.com/general/plus-model-magazine-article-detail.asp?article-id=210452787. Accessed July 3, 2008.

Rochlin, Margy. 2008. "Queen Latifah: Queen Bee. The Hardest-Working Woman in Showbiz Built an Empire without Losing Her Soul." *Reader's Digest*, October 2008, http://www.rd.com/your-america-inspiring-people-and-stories/queen-latifah-queen-bee-interview/article99958.html. Accessed December 15, 2008.

Roehling, M. V. 1999. "Weight-Based Discrimination in Employment: Psychological and Legal Aspects." *Personnel Psychology* 52: 969–1017.

Rothblum, Esther and Sondra Solovay. 2009. *The Fat Studies Reader*. New York: New York University Press.

Saguy, Abigail and Anna Ward. 2010. "Coming Out as Fat: Rethinking Stigma." *Social Psychology Quarterly* 74, 1: 53–75.

Sarkisian-Miller, Nola. 2006. "Sizing Up the Market: Premium Denim Lines Are Expanding Their Reach by Meeting the Needs of Fuller-Figured Women." *Women's Wear Daily*, January 4, 2006: 22S.

Sauers, Jenna. 2010. "Suicidal Models Are Fashion's Worst Trend." Jezebel.com, May 13, 2010, http://jezebel.com/5537856/suicidal-models-are-fashions-worst-trend. Accessed November 27, 2013.

Schwartz, Hillel. 1986. *Never Satisfied: A Cultural History of Diets, Fantasies, and Fat*. New York: Free Press.

Schwartz, Marlene B., Heather O'Neal Chambliss, et al. 2003. "Weight Bias among Health Professionals Specializing in Obesity." *Obesity Research* 11, 9: 1033–39.

Schwartz, Marlene B., Lenny R. Vartanian, et al. 2006. "The Influence of One's Own Body Weight on Implicit and Explicit Anti-Fat Bias." *Obesity* 14, 3: 440–47.

Seckler, Valerie. 2003. "Failing to Rise to Women's Size." *Women's Wear Daily*, September 24, 2003: 14.

Shaw, Hollie. 2010. "Plus-Size Lingerie Commercial Banned Because Of . . . Cleavage?" *Financial Post*, April 23, 2010, http://business.financialpost.com/2010/04/23/fp-marketing-plus-size-lingerie-commercial-banned-because-of-cleavage/. Accessed January 5, 2013.

Shilling, Chris. 1993. *The Body and Social Theory*. London; Newbury Park, CA: Sage Publications.

Shryock, Richard Harrison. 1966. "Sylvester Graham and the Popular Health Movement, 1830–1870." In *Medicine in America: Historical Essays*, 111–125. Baltimore, MD: Johns Hopkins University Press.

Simon, Nicole. 1995. "Bat Shows Potential of Plus-Size Fashions." *Women's Wear Daily*, October 26, 1995: 14.

Sims, Amy C. 2002. "Fashion's 'Big' Change?" FOX News, May 1, 2002, www.foxnews.com/printer_friendly_story/0,3566,51595,00.html. Accessed July 9, 2008.

Sobal, Jeffery. 1999. "The Size Acceptance Movement and the Social Construction of Body Weight." In *Weighty Issues: Fatness and Thinness as Social Problems*, edited by Jeffery Sobal and Donna Maurer, 231–49. Hawthorne, NY: Aldine de Gruyter.

Solovay, Sondra and Esther Rothblum. 2009. "Introduction." In *The Fat Studies Reader*, edited by Esther Rothblum and Sondra Solovay, 1–7. New York: New York University Press.

Stearns, Peter N. 1997. *Fat History: Bodies and Beauty in the Modern West*. New York: New York University Press.

Stevenson, Seth. 2005. "When Tush Comes to Dove: Real Women, Real Curves, Real Smart Ad Campaign." *Slate*, August 1, 2005, http://www.slate.com/articles/business/ad_report_card/2005/08/when_tush_comes_to_dove.html. Accessed June 1, 2008.

Stinson, Kandi M. 2001. *Women and Dieting Culture: Inside a Commercial Weight Loss Group*. New Brunswick, NJ: Rutgers University Press.

Striegel-Moore, Ruth and Linda Smolak. 2001. "Challenging the Myth of the Golden Girl: Ethnicity and Eating Disorders." In *Eating Disorders: Innovative Directions for Research and Practice*, 111–32. Washington, DC: American Psychological Association.

Taylor, Kimberly Conniff. 2006. "With Model's Death, Eating Disorders Are Again in Spotlight—Americas—International Herald Tribune." *New York Times*, November 20, 2006, http://www.nytimes.com/2006/11/20/world/americas/20iht-models.3604439.html?_r=0. Accessed October 23, 2013.

Thomas, Pattie and Carl Wilkerson. 2005. *Taking Up Space: How Eating Well and Exercising Regularly Changed My Life*. Nashville, TN: Pearlsong Press.

Vesilind, Emili. 2009. "Fashion's Invisible Woman." *Los Angeles Times*, March 1, 2009, http://articles.latimes.com/2009/mar/01/image/ig-size1. Accessed February 10, 2013.

Wacquant, Loïc. 1995. "Pugs at Work: Bodily Capital and Bodily Labour among Professional Boxers." *Body & Society* 1, 1: 65–93.

———. 2004. *Body & Soul: Notebooks of an Apprentice Boxer*. Oxford; New York: Oxford University Press.

Wainwright, Steven P. and Bryan S. Turner. 2006. "'Just Crumbling to Bits'? An Exploration of the Body, Ageing, Injury and Career in Classical Ballet Dancers." *Sociology* 40, 2: 237–55.

Wann, Marilyn. 2009. "Foreward: Fat Studies: An Invitation to Revolution." In *The Fat Studies Reader*, edited by Esther Rothblum and Sondra Solovay, ix–xxv. New York: New York University Press.

Wesely, Jennifer K. 2003. "Exotic Dancing and the Negotiation of Identity: The Multiple Uses of Body Technologies." *Journal of Contemporary Ethnography* 32, 6: 643–69.

West, Candace and Don H. Zimmerman. 1987. "Doing Gender." *Gender & Society* 1, 2: 125–51.

Weston, Michele. 2008. "My Must Agencies Hire Certain Sizes/Ages?" *Venus Diva Magazine*, http://www.venusimaging.com/Plusmodeling/Seminars/Michele/michele1.htm. Accessed March 12, 2013.

Wilson, Eric. 1997. "New Tactics in a Tough Market." *Women's Wear Daily*, September 10, 1997: 24.

————. 2012. "Checking Models' IDs at the Door." *New York Times*, February 8, 2012, http://www.nytimes.com/2012/02/09/fashion/efforts-to-stop-use-of-underage-models-during-new-york-fashion-week.html?_r=0&adxnnl=1&pagewanted=1&adxnnlx=1391281234-Szx3S3XNKMDd2vt2cCfUuA. Accessed February 1, 2014.

Wissinger, Elizabeth A. 2004. "The Value of Attention: Affective Labor in the Fashion Modeling Industry." Department of Sociology, City University of New York. Doctor of Philosophy.

Witchel, Alex. 1997. "Size 14, 190 Pounds: A Model Figure." *New York Times*, March 12, 1997, http://www.nytimes.com/1997/03/12/garden/size-14-190-pounds-a-model-figure.html. Accessed February 2, 2014.

Wolf, Naomi. 1992. *The Beauty Myth: How Images of Beauty Are Used against Women*. New York: Anchor Books.

Yadegaran McClatchy, Jessica. 2006. "Savvy, Stylish and Plus-Size." *Bismarck Tribune*, September 11, 2006, http://news.google.com/newspapers?nid=1696&dat=2006090 1&id=TAsbAAAAIBAJ&sjid=XogEAAAAIBAJ&pg=4888,341784. Accessed March 5, 2013.

Yao, Deborah. 2006. "Plus Size Becoming More Mainstream." *Washington Post*, April 23, 2006, http://www.washingtonpost.com/wp-dyn/content/article/2006/04/23/AR2006042300503.html. Accessed March 5, 2013.

Young, T. R. 1990. "Dress Drama and Self: The Tee Shirt as Text." In *The Drama of Social Life: Essays in Post-Modern Social Psychology*, 339–56. New Brunswick, NJ: Transaction Publishers.

Yuan, Jada. 2010. "Crystal Renn on Her Weight Loss, New Exercise Routine, and Walking for Karl Lagerfeld." *New York Magazine*, October 25, 2010, http://nymag.com/daily/fashion/2010/10/crystal_renn_qa.html. Accessed January 5, 2012.

ABOUT THE AUTHOR

Amanda M. Czerniawski is Assistant Professor of Sociology at Temple University.